Art by Bo (Flowers) Fowler, originally printed as stickers and distributed on the APSU Campus.

Inspiration to Action

A Tribute to Jill Eichhorn—

Professor, Activist, Peacekeeper

Foreword by
Shana Thornton

Editors
Beverly Fisher, Lee Gray,
Jennifer Goode Stevens

Thorncraft Publishing
Clarksville, Tennessee

"Counting Embodied Learning" by Dr. Jill Eichhorn first published by Demeter Press in *Counting on Marilyn Waring: New Advances in Feminist Economics*. Second Edition. Margunn Bjørnholt & Ailsa McKay, Editors (2014). Reprinted by permission from Demeter Press.

"Dear Jill" by Tami Haaland was first published in *High Country Journal*, 2023. Reprinted by permission from the author.

"The Baby Train" by Bryanna Licciardi was first published online in *Cleaver Magazine*, 2016. Reprinted by permission from the author.

Cover Design by Cindy Marsh

Book Design by Shana Thornton

ISBN-13: 978-1-961609-01-3
ISBN-10: 1-961609-01-0

Library of Congress Control Number: 2024932792

Thorncraft Publishing
Clarksville, TN 37043
https://www.thorncraftpublishing.com

10 9 8 7 6 5 4 3 2 1

For Jill

Contents

The Inspiration and Activism of Dr. Jill Eichhorn
Foreword by Shana Thornton

When Dr. Jill Eichhorn sat at the head of our graduate class table, she opened a space for her students to eat, drink, pass notes, sweep books across to one another, stack piles of notes, and dig into the challenges to our personal expressions. But perhaps more importantly, she opened the classroom so that we saw one another, could get to know one another--our differences in experience and perspective, as well as helping us to explore gender and identity theories; elbows forward, we would dig in as if devouring a meal. We read feminist texts, prepared papers, shared aloud our highs and lows, the in-between whispered parts, theories and laughter, and even too hard to handle moments when we needed to leave the classroom and breathe.

Opening to possibility was one of Jill's specialties. In the spirit of reform and impromptu techniques, she knew when it was important to say "yes" and try it out, whether in the classroom or her personal development within the community and within herself. She raised thousands of dollars for nonprofits that helped and benefited women in the Clarksville community. She used her own money to transport students to marches, rallies, and conferences in other cities. She created new classes and techniques within existing courses in the Women and Gender Studies Program at Austin Peay State University. Jill was also a perpetual student, earning her yoga teacher certification when she was over fifty and learning to play the recorder even later. She not only learned, she taught weekly yoga classes and performed music on the recorder nearly every Sunday at the Unitarian Universalist Fellowship of Clarksville. Jill was engaged whenever possible.

These pages offer testimonies about so many of Jill's strengths and achievements—some filled with grief over her passing, others written while she encouraged the creative process in person. Reading each piece was a procession, a flower laid and a heart revealed, from the people whose lives connected to hers, and even those she never met. While I read and placed each submission for the book, I shared touching memories in between with her colleagues, friends, and former students.

Dr. Cindy Marsh, who taught interdisciplinary studies courses at Austin Peay State University with Jill for years, sent files of their collaborative artwork with students from the courses, and some of those are included in this book. She also found an essay written by Jill, gifting us with Jill's words about the value of her classes, specifically *The Vagina Monologues*. The essay shows Jill's views about what she witnessed among the students in the class—their connections to one another as well as personal, creative development.

Jill's death was sudden and shocking, and her tribute book offers a balm not only from the shared stories and experiences with Jill but also with words from her. Those words point to the Women and Gender Studies Program at Austin Peay State University, and the value of that sacred space of expression and exploration. The collection opens with Jill's essay and is followed by poetry, creative monologues, essays, and tribute memories by more than thirty contributors, as well as some of the collaborative artwork with students from previous classes.

It has been my honor to carefully read and consider each tribute, to communicate about Jill, and to offer a lasting call to action from Dr. Jill Eichhorn—Professor, Activist, Peacekeeper.

Inspiration to Action

A Tribute to Jill Eichhorn—

Professor, Activist, Peacekeeper

Counting Embodied Learning: Marilyn Waring and Feminist Pedagogical Practice
Essay by Dr. Jill Eichhorn

First published by Demeter Press in *Counting on Marilyn Waring: New Advances in Feminist Economics*. Second Edition. Margunn Bjørnholt & Ailsa McKay, Editors (2014). Reprinted by permission from Demeter Press.

> "Engaged pedagogy necessarily values student expression."
> bell hooks, *Teaching to Transgress*

"My vagina's furious and it needs to talk. . . ." So begins a favorite monologue of many women who have had exposure to Eve Ensler's *The Vagina Monologues*. First performed in 1998 as a one-woman show off Broadway, Ensler's award-winning play resulted from more than 200 interviews she conducted with women from all walks of life around the world. In 2011, more than 5,800 performances were staged in forty-five countries as part of VDAY, the fundraising and political organizing arm that offers the script, staging resources and political strategy to college and community groups around the world through the website vday.org.

For the past ten years, I have used the production of the play as the central component of a women's studies course titled The Vagina Monologues. Unique in its pedagogical format, it is not a theatre course and not a traditional course with tests and papers. Instead, the course requires students to stage and perform the show, connect with the VDAY website and movement, and examine political and social conditions for women locally, nationally and internationally. Students write weekly journal responses, and the course ends with a research project and presentation on an issue for women, which might be sexual identity, body image, women's representation in the media, or an issue women face in developing countries. In existence for fourteen years, V-DAY has raised $85 million that has assisted local, regional, and international efforts to launch programs and open shelters where women can heal and transform their lives (vday.org). This international political dimension is a crucial part of students' experience. In every group I have taught, many students comment about the difference of this educational experience. They report that they feel "connected to something larger than themselves." Through the website and the documentary *VDay: Until the Violence Stops*, students understand from the first day that they are participants in a project with women around the world. But it is the unconventional course requirement of performing the play that offers students embodied learning, a learning process that includes both rational and emotional dimensions.

Marilyn Waring's *If Women Counted: A New Feminist Economics* guided me to recognize ways that patriarchal social and political structures devalued or erased practices connected to women's lives. As Gloria Steinem points out in the preface to Waring's book, "The states of female beings in general could be transformed by Waring's insistence on making reproduction finally visible as the most basic form of production" (xii). Waring's questions demonstrate how women's second-class status becomes embedded in everyday practices, resulting in normalizing women's subordination in social and political contexts. Waring's theoretical work has made me vigilant to what is invisible or devalued and led me to consider the implications of that invisibility or devaluation in my classroom practices.

Like any women's studies course, *The Vagina Monologues* course makes women's experiences visible. In particular, I count the performance of *The Vagina Monologues* as a substantial portion of the coursework. Waring's theoretical work has led me to examine how traditional patriarchal structures or frameworks frequently prevent us from seeing or valuing what the framework by design makes invisible or subordinate. Her work teaches us, for example, to consider the economic support women's unpaid labor contributes to an economy while denying women any power, status, or recognition for that labor. Focusing on international economic systems, Waring points out how water moving in pipelines has more economic value than water carried by women from wells to homes. This kind of comparison led me to examine the classroom work I assign and how that work is valued and counted. I came to understand that I had an opportunity to count the production of Ensler's play as part of students' academic development, an embodied exercise distinctive from traditional ways of engaging student development—essays, multiple choice tests, or in-class presentations or small group discussions. Performing the play is as legitimate as a paper or test, especially in the case of politically disenfranchised or marginalized groups. If "the institutions we practice in are still dominated by masculinist, Eurocentric norms of 'professional' behavior and accomplishment," as Susan Bordo argues, then when disenfranchised or marginalized groups interact with traditional institutions, only an agenda of transformation will prevent the erasure of their experience (40). Waring's analysis of international economics and the economic value denied women's work inspired me to analyze the work in the classroom and consider what and how I value student work. Through this examination, I decided to intervene in structures that privilege individualized learning, perpetuating the invisibility of women's experiences and those of other disenfranchised groups. By integrating the play's production as a major graded component in this course equivalent to a major writing assignment, I create an opportunity for a student group (outside the theatre major or minor course of study) to embody stories of women, transforming personal stories into a public narrative, now a counted visible thread in the social fabric.

Perhaps most simply, performing *The Vagina Monologues* gives students the occasion to say a word in public that is stigmatized, a word that the dictionary tells us is "the passage leading from the opening of the vulva to the cervix of the uterus in female mammals" (1488). Yet, clearly, a taboo surrounds the word. Ensler recounts in her memoir that when she began performing the monologues, "[she] realized that just saying the word 'vagina' caused enormous controversy, because 'vagina' is, in fact, the most isolated, reviled word in any language. You can find words like 'nuclear,' 'scud,' or 'plutonium' on the front pages of newspapers and they never cause anywhere near such a stir" (74). Students report similar experiences talking to friends, family, and teachers about the course. One male professor on our campus told a student that he supported the concept of ending violence against women, but found it problematic that the play's title uses a "dirty" word.

In explaining how the cultural taboo around the word "vagina" works, Ensler writes,

> The taboo on the word is no accident. As long as we cannot say "vagina," vaginas do not exist. They remain isolated and unprotected. Young girls get genitally mutilated and sex-trafficked throughout the world. Women get raped, burned with acid, and beaten, and no one is held accountable. (75)

Ensler's observations about how the word "vagina" operates in discourse motivates her to transform the value and meaning of the word.

While she attempts to intervene in culture through the vehicle of her play, some scholars challenge Ensler's use of the word. It is problematic, one scholar argues, in accepting the identification of woman as linked with the word, "vagina." Kim Hall warns, "The vagina, like the category 'woman,' is a political category" (113). Following the thinking of Monique Wittig, Hall outlines the limitations of reducing the definition of woman to the capacity of giving birth. Hall argues that "to engage in the project of reclaiming the vagina without simultaneously adopting a strategy of disidentification regarding the reality of the vagina does not challenge the social, political, historical, and economic context that imbues the vagina with meaning" (113). However, in Middle Tennessee, where some students timidly sign up for women's studies courses and whisper about feminist politics, participation in *The Vagina Monologues* is a step in a process of unlearning patriarchal thinking. If the play reinscribes patriarchal concepts about being female, the venues of the theatre and the classroom can offer opportunities to participate in conversations about the way the play universalizes representations of women's experiences inaccurately. Political analysis aside, the play responds to the experience many students report, that saying the word violates an invisible social contract, and symbolically the word carries connotations of what it means to be female. For student performers and audiences of the play both on and off campus, *The Vagina Monologues* creates a space where women's experiences matter, where their bodies are not sexually objectified, and their interests are not narrowly collapsed into sexual objectification, shopping, marriage, or children.

To address the significance of performing the play and of moving from invisibility to visibility, from silence to voice, I frame here three beginnings: Eve Ensler's beginnings with performing the play, students' beginnings with their performances, and my own beginnings in finding my voice. In each story of beginnings, a transformation occurs related to speaking the word "vagina" in a public space. These stories chronicle the necessary transformation of an individual to recognize her power and begin to use it. As feminist theatre educators Elizabeth Armstrong and Kathleen Juhl comment, "By expanding definitions of pedagogy...we acknowledge that artistic work frequently generates paradigm shifts, creating consciousness-raising that changes the way we see ourselves and society" (8). Counting the performance of *The Vagina Monologues* as equivalent to an essay or test in the system of higher education allows female students to feel that their emotional growth matters, students whose experience as females is traditionally marginalized and subordinated in the academic agenda. Through this act, I expand the range of projects with which students engage and create the possibility of the paradigm shifts Ensler, my students, and I have experienced.

Beginnings I

Eve Ensler's own transformation fueled by her performance of the play as a one-woman show is revealed in her introduction to *The Vagina Monologues*:

> Almost 15 years have passed since I first said the word 'vagina' on a small stage in a little theater called HERE in downtown New York City. When I first read these monologues, my most pressing concern was being able to get the words out of my terrified mouth. I certainly could not have conceived then what would follow in terms of both a movement to end violence against women and girls, and the life of *The Vagina Monologues* itself.

More significantly, she explains, "Saying the word I was not supposed to say is the thing that gave me a voice in the world. Revealing the very personal stories of women and their private parts gave birth to a public, global movement to end violence against women and girls called V-Day" (xi-xii). Here, Ensler charts how speaking the word "vagina" in public challenges a social and political framework that subordinates and silences female experiences and perspectives.

This transformation Ensler identifies in herself and the birth of the V-Day movement is connected to the venue of the theater. She writes, "Theater...allows us, it encourages us, as a community of strangers, to go someplace together and face the issues and realities we simply cannot face alone. Alone, we are powerless, translating our suffering and struggle into our own private narcissistic injuries. When we become a group, these issues become social or political concerns, responsibilities, a reason for being here together" (75). When Ensler first performed the monologues, women would line up after performances to tell her their stories of abuse and violation. Because of their stories, Ensler gathered a group of celebrities and political activists to ask the question: How do we use this play as a catalyst to end violence against women? Out of that meeting, V-Day was born.

Observing how the word "vagina" was valued and questioning those appraisals, Ensler asked women how they felt about the word. Her questions opened women's silence to voice their experiences of pain, humor, humiliation, joy, and celebration. Just as Waring reveals the subordination of women's work in international economic structures, Ensler asked a question that shows how the word vagina is devalued in contrast to other words, posing the question in a way that generated stories to see and experience a connotation contrary to the mainstream culture's pejorative or embarrassed regard for it. "By saying 'vagina' often enough and loud enough in places where it was not supposed to be said," Ensler writes, "we made the saying of it both political and mystical and gave birth to a worldwide movement to end violence against women" (72). By speaking the word and stories about vaginas, Ensler transformed the culture to value what was once devalued or silenced.

Beginnings II

On the first day of class, I ask students to interview each other to break down the barriers of individualized experience in the classroom and encourage students to connect with each other, but I am also conducting informal research. Students are instructed to ask each other why they are taking this course. Frequently, students report that a friend recommended the course as one that is different and rewarding. In a similar vein, students claim that they learn about who they are as women. In other words, their experiences as women carry value as a central component of the course. These student stories emerged in a format similar to Ensler's through which she generated the material to write her play. My students were asked: Describe your perception of yourself before taking *The Vagina Monologues* course and before performing the play on stage. Secondly, students were prompted: Describe changes, if any, in how you perceive yourself that you attribute to your participation in the course or in the stage production. While the monologues as a whole create necessarily reductive generalizations of women's experience, students' testimonies demonstrate that performing in the play and discussing the issues the play generates constitute a path of agency and voice, as Ensler recounts in her own journey. Performing in the play offers an alternative to sitting in silence and isolation. One student reported, "Before the class, I never participated in discussions." She said she routinely doubted that she had anything significant to add to a conversation. Throughout her student life, she listened to classmates speak, judging that her classmates were more "well-spoken" than she. After the course, she reflected that she understood that "everyone has their unique voice," and "every voice is valuable to what needs to be learned." This student transformed from one who sat passively in classroom discussions, perceiving other students as better able to articulate ideas, to feeling the value of adding her voice to any public discussion.

Another student commented that the act of saying aloud the words in the narrative titled "The Flood" taught her "how important words can be and how important a person's experience can be." This student's experience of learning through doing identifies a dimension of performing the show categorized as kinesthetic or embodied learning. The student remarked on a quality of understanding that she did not have before performing the show, and in particular, speaking the story of the flood aloud in public space. In the university environment, reading and writing are privileged as modes of learning over visual and kinesthetic learning. Recognizing a wide range of learning styles is standard practice in the Montessori and Waldorf models, and in the Suzuki method of learning musical instruments. In education courses, future teachers are coached to engage different styles of learning as they plan how to expose their students to new material and ideas. And yet, at the university level, outside the disciplines in the arts, students' self expression is muted through coaching a disembodied writing voice that is meant to report information or formulate arguments with objective or universal authority. This student's experience shows that speaking words aloud facilitates a kind of understanding that is difficult to quantify.

Evaluating both her professional and emotional development, one student said, "During the first production in 2002, I did not imagine that I would ever be an alumnus of a university, and I did not imagine that I would be faculty, but today, I am both. I used to believe I was a strong woman, that I had my place in the world. Looking back on it now, I learned that I had room to grow, lots of room to grow." Personally, she described a growth in her voice. "I used to believe I had a voice, but in performing *The Vagina Monologues,* I found a new, stronger voice that I am still getting acquainted with after all this time—singing. I began to sing, and then I began to change for the better." Here the student uses "singing" metaphorically to describe a transformation in the quality of her voice, a stronger voice.

Students recognized their own voices becoming stronger, and they recognized how they might advocate for other women. One student reported that she learned that she could be an advocate for women, but more importantly, she said, "I could be an advocate for myself. I could give myself a voice in a positive, constructive way." She claimed more confidence in herself and increased comfort in her body image. "I credit 'the monologues'" for that transformation, she said. "Getting on stage," she explained, was terrifying, and yet it gave her a sense of "power." Finally, she commented that on stage she felt "a kind of strength that I didn't know I had before."

"I surprised myself in what I could actually do," reported another student. Another commented, "I found a part of myself that I didn't know was there." And finally, a student reported that she can now say "vagina" without blushing.

The performers grow, and the audience grows. Following a performance one year, a woman wrote me and thanked me for the opportunity to experience the play. She had been a student at our university for seven years and only this particular year had an opportunity to see the show. At the end of the show, we invite the cast and the audience to stand if they are a survivor of violence so that the audience can honor them. Half of the cast stood up, a few in the audience. The student who wrote me said she summoned the courage to count herself as a survivor and that by standing up she transformed feeling victimized by her experience into feeling that she had survived it. She wrote that she felt "free" of it. This is the alchemy of theatre that Eve Ensler describes, an alchemy that affects both the people in the cast and the audience. To speak the suffering, to take a symbolic stand in public, to acknowledge one's silent or invisible suffering embodies the experience. Through this embodiment, creating the paradigm shift from silence to sound, the experience is transformed.

Performers grow, audience members grow, and students as directors grow. Part of V-Day's vision is that *The Vagina Monologues* provides leadership opportunities for women. The VDAY rules offer the script without royalty fees as long as students direct the show and coordinate the publicity. One student story follows her experience of first performing in the show and then directing a show the next year. Before taking the course and performing in the show, she described herself as "terrified completely of talking to two people in a group." However, because "everyone supported each other to have their voice heard in and out of class," this student accomplished taking the stage and delivering her lines. She acknowledged *The Vagina Monologues* course and performance experience as the catalyst that improved her ability to speak in public. In fact, the next year, she took charge of directing an alumni/faculty show. In that performance she chose to read all of the introductions to the monologues. Because of this experience, she said, she had confidence that she could "put something together, get it done, and succeed at it." She concluded that she "cannot think of any other situation where I would have gotten this kind of opportunity."

In the V-Day documentary, Jane Fonda says that she believes that "it is fitting that women are transforming through art." More than fitting, I might assert that women transform because of the artistic context, where emotions and wholeness of experience inspire women, as Armstrong and Juhl point out, to see themselves in new ways.

Beginnings III

In 2001, one of my students, a theatre major, saw *The Vagina Monologues* in San Francisco and returned insisting that we perform the play on campus. I was speechless. Untenured, I was completely unnerved by the prospect of producing this play about women's sexuality. The student talked to a tenured social work professor, who taught human sexuality, and a tenured drama professor. They asked me if I wanted to join them in offering a course which we would teach together, bringing in speakers addressing issues the play raised and producing the show as part of the course. The student discovered the College Campaign, V-Day, which offered the script to student groups free of royalties if the play was used to raise money for local agencies that assist women and girls who are survivors of violence. On February 14, 2002, Austin Peay State University was one of 514 campuses in V-Day's College Campaign hosting *The Vagina Monologues* APSU's 600-seat Clement Auditorium was packed, raising $2,000 in two performances.

In 2002, Clarksville's Roxy Regional Theatre produced the show, where my student was asked to direct it. I wanted to be brave enough to perform. But, I have to admit that I was intimidated. I wanted to face my fear without letting it paralyze me—and on some level, I did not even understand how paralyzed and frozen I was, just beginning my interior journey of unlocking my personal history of sexual violation. Somewhere around this time, I picked up one of those quotable magnets with words from Eleanor Roosevelt: "You gain strength, courage, and confidence by every experience in which you really stop to look fear in the face...Do the thing you think you cannot do." Part of me did not believe that I could perform those monologues on stage as I had watched my students do without making a fool of myself. And yet, how could I ask them to do what I myself feared?

Their courage inspired me. My voice occasionally quaked. My insides trembled as I sat on stage. Facing my terror, finding my way into the rhythm of the words, sharing the stage with actresses and my colleagues helped me see myself differently. As Armstrong and Juhl suggest about feminist theatre experience, my paradigm shifted, altering my image of myself. My children, who were 12 and 7 at the time, and my partner delighted to hear me swear in public. I delighted to hear myself swear in public. I delighted in the transgressive act, expressing guttural, embodied, "not-taking-shit" swearing. Finding this grounded anger through the words and expressing them in public transformed my anger and feelings of victimization from my own violations. What I have come to understand through teaching this course and other women's studies courses is that even for girls and women who have not suffered a personal physical or sexual violation, there is the violation of the media that teaches boys and men to objectify women as it teaches girls and women to objectify themselves. There is no female in the modern world who escapes it. The play, however, offers a public, communal response to the media's efforts to objectify us, for both performers and audience. Women on stage or in the audience learn to transform the way we see ourselves from victims to survivors, from objects to subjects. Our voices join the women's experiences in the play, and together our voices interrupt the silence with sounds and stories women recognize.

That transformation for me has meant that I now teach the course on my own, a professor who has earned tenure. My courage to speak the truths of sexual and physical violation and to listen to students' stories of violation has grown as I have been involved with performing, producing this play, and teaching the issues and questions the play generates. Performing in the play is not a substitute for therapy, but, as one woman, Laura, in the V-Day documentary explains, talking about violation in the private space of therapy is a different experience than creating the quilt she made about her own violation and restrictions in her teens (VDay). Making the quilt and speaking about the experience in public shifts the story from the private domain to the public where the weight of the suffering is at least lessened. In some cases, it disappears. For many women, the shame is so crippling, it silences us. The public ritual of narrating our own experience or a similar one lifts the shame and isolation and frees us to fill the silence with our own sound, our embodied and empowered voices.

I no longer feel fear anticipating my performance at the Roxy. I have performed in three shows each season for ten years. I believe working with this play, with the students, and learning their stories has shown me the importance of the process to all of us, in all of our diversity of experience. As part of the course, we address body image, racial and ethnic identities, sexual identities and orientation, birth and menstruation, images of women in the media, particularly Sut Jhally's documentary, *Dreamworlds III*. The study of these subjects deepens the transformation the play stimulates.

Other course components are unconventional as I introduce the discipline of the theater process. To value the process of the play, I schedule the auditions, one rehearsal, and the final show during class time. I work with a student population that juggles going to school full-time and one or two jobs. I use the class time (once a week for three hours) to build in the process they would experience for a dramatic production. Many students have never been on stage before. Frequently students are coming to terms with violations or abusive relationships for the first time, as they are exposed to information that pushes them to examine their personal worlds. On the first day of class, I inform each female student that she will have some part in the show. She only has to say one word, and she doesn't have to be on stage alone, but each female member of the course has to get on stage. I make this requirement after observing for several years students who were reluctant to get on stage, but who challenged themselves to perform. I observed their nervousness and timidity before the show, and then their joy and self-confidence after facing the challenge and transforming through the process. By contrast, I observed students who, fearing to get on stage, were allowed to sit in their fear. Their fear imprisoned them. They still enjoyed the course and the experience, but their relationship to the group and to the experience was different from the experience of those who performed. As Ensler indicates, "the alchemy of theatre," the process and ritual of going through the show, changes each performer. To place the performance of the play as a central project in my course opens a space to see and experience the connotation of the word *vagina* differently. By extension, the connotations of being female in this patriarchal culture expand and allow women to find versions of themselves who demand, for example, as one woman states in the VDay documentary, "rape-free zones."

2001 marked the beginning of my odyssey with teaching a course that created time, space, networking, resources, and critical engagement with the topics generated by Eve Ensler's *The Vagina Monologues*. Many women who have experienced the performance—in the audience or on stage—have reported the transformative potential of the play. There is a deeper transformation when the play is part of an academic course, where the play transforms the traditionally patriarchal paradigm that privileges male experience over female experience. When the play offers participants—directing, performing, or listening—the opportunity to develop confidence, the emotions discovered and expressed create a crucible for women's power. When women embody their voices, they express their autonomy. When women see themselves as autonomous subjects, they transform their relationship to power.

An exam, a multiple-choice test, a personal essay, a research paper—these forms of academic work offer students a particular kind of individualized intellectual experience and growth. As professors and instructors, we evaluate this growth through grades, a ritual that counts and quantifies student progress and learning leading toward an academic degree. These forms of evaluation privilege individualized learning, and this kind of learning context values a particular kind of intellectual ability. Waring's work asks us to count women's contributions in international economic frameworks. Eve Ensler's play asks us to count and value women's gendered experiences. Taking the lead of these two activists who challenge us to imagine and create a world where women's work and experience count, I place the performance of Eve Ensler's *The Vagina Monologues* at the heart of an academic course as a graded component, and by doing so I honor the courage female students summon to announce in public space that their experiences as women matter, and their efforts to narrate these stories as a group in a public forum constitute a legitimate measure of their learning.

Works Cited

American Heritage Dictionary. Third Ed. New York: Houghton Mifflin, 1997. Print.

Armstrong, Elizabeth and Kathleen Juhl. Eds. Introduction. *Radical Acts: Theatre and Feminist Pedagogies of Change*. San Francisco: aunt lute books, 2007. Print.

Bordo, Susan. *Unbearable Weight: Feminism, Western Culture, and the Body*. Berkley, CA: U of California P, 1993. Print.

Ensler, Eve. *The Vagina Monologues. Tenth Anniversary Edition*. New York: Villard, 2008. Print.

Hall, Kim Q. "Queerness, Disability, and *The Vagina Monologues*." *Hypatia* 20.1 (Winter 2005): 100-116. *Literature Resource Center*. Web. Oct. 10, 2011.

hooks, bell. *Teaching to Transgress: Education as the Practice of Freedom*. New York: Routledge, 1994. Print.

Steinem, Gloria. *Counting for Nothing: What Men Value and What Women are Worth*. By Marilyn Waring. Toronto, U of Toronto P, 1999. Print.

VDay: Until the Violence Stops. Dir. Abby Epstein. New Video Group, 2005. Film.

VDay: A Global Movement to Stop Violence Against Women and Girls. http://www.vday.org. Web. 25 March 2012.

Waring, Marilyn. *Counting for Nothing: What Men Value and What Women are Worth*. Second Edition. Toronto: U of Toronto P, 1999. Print.

Dear Jill
Poetry by Tami Haaland

Dear Jill—
Where to begin? Snow on the ground now,
but I still miss summer. One evening in August,
nighthawks filled the sky, dozens swooping
and diving like swallows over a river. I see
this neighborhood as flowering grasses along
an irrigation ditch, a fox standing in the road,
five deer who graze on hillsides in all seasons,
even a single sighting of racoon near the cliffs
that border our northern horizon. Houses blend
to background. Once I found a crow head and scatter
of feathers, prey to great horned owls who prowl
trees and sky until dawn. In this year's isolation,
I learned where ravens nest. How I had failed to understand
still amazes me. Or the mourning dove's eye.
Did you know a blue ring surrounds it, and feathers
along its throat shine with salmon-colored iridescence?
Maybe this is the best part of years passing, learning
to look and look again at a young marmot, a nuthatch,
blue jays in a half-downed cottonwood. When you call
we pick up as if time has not passed. Certain moments—
the moon rising over Flathead when we stayed
at Liz's cabin—come back, but I won't turn sentimental.
Let's not wait long to take the road trip we've
imagined. I want one of those tents that opens
to the stars, and my car can get us where we need
to go. Last August I sat beneath aspens and thought of you.
Cicadas razzed above me and I noticed how they wound
down to a mild hum, then a pause, and when I thought
they had nothing more to say, they launched again.
                    As always, Tami

Gifts
Nonfiction by Susan Calovini

The sudden and stunning death of Jill Eichhorn left many of us seeking solace in our memories, perhaps in stories about happy times spent with Jill, or in the gifts that she bestowed on us. Generous and thoughtful, a brilliant and dedicated teacher, a loyal and supportive friend, Jill gave her students, colleagues, and friends many intangible gifts—gifts of her spirit, knowledge, wisdom, passion, love. I am thinking now, however, of some of the tangible gifts she gave me and the ways in which they continue to speak to me with her voice, sometimes inspiring and strengthening, always comforting.

I had the good fortune to know Jill from the time she came to Clarksville. Indeed, I knew of her before she arrived. During his campus interview for a faculty position in creative writing at Austin Peay State University, Barry Kitterman arranged to meet me privately to discuss the then-Women's Studies Program, which I directed at the time, and to ask about opportunities for Jill to contribute to the program should he be offered the job. I was thrilled to learn about the possibility of adding a strong feminist scholar-teacher to our community and of having her as my colleague in Women's Studies as well as in English. Although Jill began at APSU in a part-time teaching role when Barry accepted the job, within a few years our department was fortunate to offer her a full-time tenure-track position, and I was pleased that Jill agreed to lead Women's Studies as I moved into the department chair office. Going forward, she demonstrated that she was the right person to direct it. She improved the program by including an advocacy element along with the scholarly curriculum and by broadening the overall focus to incorporate Gender Studies. Speaking of gifts, she was truly a "gift" to the APSU Women's and Gender Studies Program and its students.

Through the years that we worked together, and beyond, Jill gifted me with a number of tokens of her friendship and affection. I suspect that she was more thoughtful in this way than I was, but I am unashamedly grateful for her gifts. Three especially have frequently been in my mind since her passing. Poignant yet comforting, these three have come to symbolize for me important aspects of Jill's personality and character that I deeply admire.

When I open the kitchen cupboard every morning to reach for my tea mug, my eyes also light on a small ceramic bowl that was a birthday present from Jill long ago. Until my recent retirement, it sat on various desks or bookshelves in various offices during my career in academia. Now it is at home with me. It is an especially lovely bowl in the way that it balances two kinds of beauty, two opposing values. The inside is lustrous with a smooth black glaze that also extends around the outer rim in a shiny ebony ring. The outside of the bowl, in contrast, is predominantly unglazed beige clay featuring tiny black specks and a rough texture. Descending from the upper rim, four small black figures reminiscent of birds, flowers, and leaves are incised in the clay, adding a polished touch to that everyday exterior. The artist's initials and a date (1997) are etched on the bottom. How like Jill, I think as I look at this bowl—not only in its Asian influence, reminding me of her time spent in China and Taiwan, but also in its blending of the elegant and the earthy, the formal and the casual, art and craft. Jill was as comfortable when dressed in a flowing scarf or vibrant silk jacket as she was in khaki pants and hiking shoes. She looked great no matter what she was wearing, and it was hard (even for a friend) not to envy the beauty of her makeup-free face, her thick silvering hair, or that remarkable smile. Her aesthetic standards are expressed in this delicate bowl and remind me of how much she appreciated the beautiful things of the world from art, colors, and nature to, of course, literature.

The bowl "speaks" to me through its imagery, but other gifts bear her written words, her actual voice. One is a greeting card that I keep on top of my dresser now, a daily message from Jill. Her handwriting inside wishes me "joy" and "love" on some birthday many years ago, but it is the picture on the front that most moves me. There, a black and white photograph shows five women caught momentarily in a dance pose, all standing on one leg with their hands joined and heads turned to their right, forming a line across the photo. What is striking about the image is not their ballet pose but the dancers themselves, who are far from typical ballerinas. The five women are diverse in every visible way, including age, race, body size, clothing, and hairstyle. Black and white, young and old, tall and short, barefooted and slippered, wearing old-fashioned house dresses, flowing skirts, or blue jeans, and with their auburn or gray hair swept up or flowing down—these women clasp hands with each other, arms laced in front of their waists, and perform their steps with a uniform look of ease, seriousness, and pleasure. The back of the card informs me that they are members of the Liz Lerman Dance Exchange, "a company of performers whose ages span six decades," and that the purchase of this card supports the Syracuse Cultural Workers, an organization "which inspires and sustains efforts to achieve social and environmental justice, liberation, equality and peace." In the vital causes it supports and in its depiction of diverse women joined together in serious endeavor, of women mutually supporting each other in "the dance" of life, of artists bringing beauty and joy into the world, this card conveys many of the values and beliefs that Jill Eichhorn espoused. Seeing it each day feels a bit like having a conversation with her, and I often think something like "yes, Jill, yes" before leaving the room where it is displayed.

Her written words are also part of the third gift I have kept close to me during this past year. It is a text that Jill sent to me four days before her death. Knowing that she was in the hospital facing the shocking news of her diagnosis, I had sent a message of concern and support, hardly expecting a response from her at all, or at least not anytime soon. When she texted back eleven minutes later, it was with words of love and thoughtfulness towards me. Reminding me of our last phone call in late July, just a few months earlier, she wrote that she "loved our conversation this summer" and peppered her text with her signature strings of red hearts. Every time I read it now, I am unfailingly moved by her ability to think about me—to think about anyone but her own self—in that time of personal crisis. Her kindness and empathy were so much a part of who she was.

I also appreciate the way her message takes me back to our July phone call, when our talk about friends, family, work, and retirement led to the revelation that we both had begun memorizing poems in recent months or years. We were tickled by this connection and promised to memorize one of each other's favorite poems as a way of cementing this newfound bond. I sent her a link to Li Young Li's carpe diem poem, "From Blossoms," which Jill called "so lovely." And she shared with me her choice: Joy Harjo's "Eagle Poem." This eloquent, prayer-like work about the circle of life, about our human connections with the natural world, and about the desire to live a life of "beauty" has become part of the mental repertoire of poems that I recite to myself in quiet moments or during my daily walks. It inspires me not only to remember Jill but also to contemplate its timeless message about life's brevity and how best to live.

Jill's life and death will not soon be forgotten by those who knew her. She gave constantly and fruitfully of herself to the world around her—by loving her family, educating her students, and supporting her colleagues, community, and friends. I am grateful for her numerous gifts to me, tangible and intangible. I am deeply grateful for the gift of her friendship.

Natural Woman
For Jill
Poetry by Mitzi Cross

When the Sun entered
Leo on August 1st, 1957,
a rebel was born
with a fire in her belly
and a wanderlust that would take
her away from her small life
in Gary, Indiana.

She was a girl,
on the edge of womanhood,
with her sun-kissed shoulders,
and dusty, skinned-up knees.
She liked to walk the shallow
creek bed gathering heart-shaped
rocks, as her wind-tangled hair
blew wildly across her brown eyes.
Eyes that would witness
the mountain ranges and water-
colored skyscapes of Montana,
the flat, green, vista, of Ohio
and all the way across the world
to teach in China.
She never imagined
the adventures she would have,
like being a mother, which she
proclaimed as her greatest creation.

She would not acknowledge
she was a healer, as she moved
yoga students through Asanas or
opened her classroom to confessions
and the unburdening of pain. She

created a safe Fort where childhood
wounds could be uncovered, the bruises

of abuse she would witness and
carry them back into the light.
She was an illuminator of the Sun
and all who knew her were brightened
by her presence.

Every Woman Should Be a Feminist
Nonfiction by Lachon Sumers

Every woman should be a feminist. Growing up, I assumed that feminism was a white woman's thing. That Black women didn't have the luxury to be a feminist. That Black women had other struggles to deal with and that my race came before my gender. The truth is that Black women aren't taught about the importance of us all being feminist. Some Black women at a young age aren't taught important Black women leaders through the waves of feminism. Feminism doesn't belong to a race or a certain demographic. It is a practice that anyone who cares about a woman should care about.

Being raised in the South, going to Title I schools feminism education was not a part of the curriculum. I was taught African American history by a book during February. In high school when the women's suffrage movement was discussed, it was hard for me to understand the importance of feminism. In our class discussions, Black women were not mentioned as impactful leaders in the women's suffrage movement. Black women were only in the curriculum when slavery was taught. If they were taught, it was Harriet Tubman, Rosa Parks, or Sojourner Truth—all important women, but only the tip of the iceberg of impactful women in the Black feminist community.

It wasn't until my years in college that I was blessed to be taught about the history of feminism. I wasn't open-minded about the course because of the past, however my instructor changed my entire perception of feminism. One fall, I signed up for my first feminism course, as my minor—African American Studies—required students to take a course within Women and Gender Studies. Dr. Eichhorn was my introduction into all things feminism.

Most of my peers who have had Dr. Eichhorn informed me of her brilliance—recognizing her as the color purple, which made me keep my eyes open on campus. Once the semester began, I was excited to join the class and learn more about the importance of feminism. The course discussions ranged from feminism waves.

Vagina is a word that we used so freely in the class. I was very hesitant to continue to say the word. To discuss our learning of our periods. How some of our mothers were uncomfortable discussing our periods. Or how our peers hid their periods out of fear. How the moon was a beautiful factor in our menstruating. The safety that came with having the space to be women. Although there was one male in our class, he listened and learned just as I did.

Dr. Eichhorn gave my peers and me the reassurance we needed to be comfortable. She shared with us that our stories were safe and that being a feminist is the best thing a woman could be. That being a feminist is for everyone. There was no shape, skin color, age, job description that came to respecting and acknowledging that women were women. She shared her story with us. Some classes were silent, others were filled with laughter, and all were a safe haven for feminists.

Everyone should be a feminist, but not because if you identify as a woman it's the right thing to do. Everyone should be a feminist because women are so many things all at once.

Women are the light that seeps through the blinds.

Women are the backbone of everyone's success.

Women are the universe.

Women are the wind that glides through the wind chimes.

Women are the song you can't get out of your head.

Women are humans.

I thank God for placing the beautiful angel that was and still is Dr. Jill Eichhorn—for being the beautiful, eclectic, vagina warrior she was to so many different people on campus. Thank you for teaching me that every woman should be a feminist.

Tick Tock Metronome
Poetry by Dr. Mickey Wadia

She's a pendulum. A metal rod that swings
back and forth.
a resolute and steadfast timekeeper.
like a tireless windshield wiper
that ticks and tocks with each swing
providing a steady, constant beat.

A large static weight at the end producing
click sounds that mark tempo and the pace of our lives.
She easily breaks down complex polyrhythms
Into smaller comprehensible sections.
Helps us know when we're consciously
speeding up or slowing down.

She hears our hearts and our collective conscience
and asks us to re-evaluate our code,
our standards, and our scruples.
Never quick to judge
our choices, our actions, or our indolence
her winders and gears always in good working order
programmed to respond.

Her casing was not made of plastic or wood.
Instead, it was always kindness, love, and laughter.
A hug, an embrace, a kind word
aiding us to make empathic choices and
foster understanding and instill tolerance
for the ones who sometimes missed the beat,
falling into improper rhythms and moving out of tempo.

She watches over us, keeping track of our clicks and cautions us
gently when we go astray
making poor choices
and flawed decisions at the end of the day.
An exemplary advocate for the value of humans,
we relied on her steadfast compass in times of sadness and joy
to show us the way of a windshield, not the rear-view mirror.

———————————————

We will forever miss the comforting tick tock
of our own human metronome.
Our beloved Jill Eichhorn.

The Magic in Us All
Nonfiction by Cindy Chambers

"Whatever you can do, or dream you can do, begin it: Boldness has genius, power, and magic in it."
~ Johann Wolfgang von Goethe

The first time Jill Eichhorn played the recorder at our little Unitarian Universalist congregation, blowing her first tentative notes into that instrument of torture, I had a flashback.

I could see my fourth-grade music teacher moving from student to student, handing each of us a recorder from a battered cardboard box. Mine had tooth marks on the mouthpiece, a silent testament to a now-ancient fourth-grader's frustration. The tooth marks made sense: The recorder, as I quickly discovered, is an unforgiving instrument. Unless you blow just so...unless your fingers are perfectly positioned...the resulting sound can only be described as a cross between an angry cat and a happy duck. The combination is truly squirm-worthy.

And yes, we squirmed a bit at Jill's first notes, gazing uncomfortably at the Unitarian fellowship banner behind her, its rainbowed symbol reminding us that we are an open and loving congregation. Because Jill's first solo was very much like my own. The only difference was that mine was performed in my bedroom, the door firmly shut, with only a much-kissed poster of the Beatles to witness my musical ineptitude.

Yet when Jill finished her painfully long thirty-second performance, she appeared...unperturbed. Satisfied even.

Still, I thought this would be the first and last time she would play for us. Turns out I didn't really know Jill Eichhorn.

What she might have lacked in natural ability, she made up for in dogged determination. Every Sunday, dressed in sensible sandals and cargo shorts or flowing skirt, Jill would step up and serenade us on the recorder. The accompaniment of our talented pianist helped; like frosting on a somewhat imperfect cake, he smoothed the finished product and made it more palatable.

And over the course of weeks and months, her performances grew less squirm-worthy. There were far fewer squawks and squeals, until, at last, there were none. I began looking forward to her performances, knowing they would add just the right notes to a religious tradition that celebrates uncertainty and discovery.

We all marveled when Jill took her place beside the piano on Sunday, September 25, 2022. From determination grew confidence; from confidence grew ability. She played beautifully, liltingly, bathed in a glow from the windows behind her, seemingly transported to a world where anything is possible if you just dream you can do it.

Exactly one week later, she was gone.

Goethe was right: Boldness has genius. Boldness has power. Boldness has magic. Jill Eichhorn was bold. She taught us all to embrace the joyful imperfection of growth...one magical note at a time.

Autumn Requiem
For Jill
Poetry by Joanna Grisham

Autumn now, and the leaves skitter across sidewalks
like noisy children running from the wind, toward

an invisible joy. Lawns forget their green, drape
themselves in crunchy-brown blankets, prepare

for the cold nights to come. Trees let go
of their vanity, revealing what they always were

underneath the frills: sturdy, but not immovable,
not immune to breaking when the winds pick up. I walk

the loop of my neighborhood and think of you, stolen
like breath after a too-hard fall, your purple vest, silver

hair, voice soothing like the lavender you smoothed
onto my wrists to help me breathe before a big exam,

imagine you in a dusty classroom, book in hand, bearing
your whole heart every day, showing your students

the stakes, the obligation, how to learn from the past,
remake ourselves in the morning. It's almost Halloween.

Porches are lined with pumpkins, soon to bare
crooked smiles alit with something like horror

or hope. Children will cover their faces with masks, pretend
to be terrifying, become their own fears, safely for one

night. Someday they will learn the real nightmare is not
some vampire, bedtime monster, or even death. It's love.

Kindness Knows No Bounds: A Reflection of My Time with
Jill Eichhorn
Nonfiction by Courtney Woodard

Kindness is a word that I have always associated with Dr. Jill
Eichhorn. To her friends, family, colleagues, and even to students,
she was known as Jill. The feminist icon she was, you didn't need
to say her last name, everyone knew who you were referring to
when you said "Jill." I remember my first meeting with her as an
Austin Peay State University freshman. She once again
introduced herself as Jill, and I remember thinking how cool it
was that a professor let students use her first name. She was
wearing her signature purple outfit—a light purple sweater vest,
dark purple pants, and purple socks with Birkenstock shoes.
Right away, I knew this was someone I wanted to know
personally. Her words carried wisdom and tranquility. She always
had time to connect with students on a personal level and cared
about their lives outside of the classroom. Though my time with
her was short, her kindness reached me, nonetheless.

In my first year at APSU, I took the Introduction to Women's
and Gender Studies course. There, I was introduced to feminist
teachings that would shape my perspective of the world. It was
also during this time I began to see that the current relationship I
was involved in was extremely unhealthy. With guidance from Jill
and her resources, I was able to leave the relationship and begin
my healing process. Reflecting on that time of my life now, I am
unsure if I would have left the relationship in good health had I
not been exposed to Jill and her teachings. It was a traumatic
experience, but one that I have grown from thanks to Jill.

During the last two years of my time at APSU, I spent a lot of
time with Jill working in the Feminist Majority Leadership
Alliance (FMLA). In the spring of 2019, she invited me to FMLA's
annual trip to the Young Feminist Leadership Conference in
Washington, D.C. Jill drove about ten students in a van the entire
way there and back. I told her not to worry, and that I had my

rosary on hand if needed. She laughed and responded that she had prayed to the goddess as well for a safe journey. I remember thinking that if Jill had asked for safe passage, then we would be in good hands. That same semester, FMLA began holding more events including one event titled "Spill the Tea." As I explained that "spill the tea" was slang for gossip, Jill was confused as to why anyone would waste tea, as tea was good for the body's digestion. Eventually, we got her to use the term correctly. She was always willing to learn from others, even if it was about slang terms.

The academic year of 2019-2020 was the year I saw Jill's kindness play out in real time. In 2019, Jill received the APSU Distinguished Community Service Award, an award she more than deserved. Instead of using the money for herself, she used it to purchase tickets for FMLA to attend an event headlined by Gloria Steinem. I and other feminists were able to hear from a feminist icon as well as meet others who shared our passion for equality. Again, Jill could have used this money for herself but decided to share it with her students instead. That was the kind of person she was. She always put others first, no matter the cost to herself. Jill also spread her work into the African American Studies Department by collaborating with the infamous Dr. Dwonna Goldstone on several projects. The most prominent project was the joint Capstone course between the African American Studies and Women's and Gender Studies programs that helped students create connections and advance their skills before graduation. Thanks to Jill and Dr. Goldstone, I used the skills from this course to progress into my professional career, just as I know other students did.

There were several moments when her kindness reached me personally, and not just as a student. In my final semester, she collaborated with my academic advisor to create an entirely new internship so that I could work with her. I think about this moment often. At the time I did not know she had to advocate for me to have this position. I just knew that it was approved one day, and I began working with her. Later, I found that she had argued on my behalf to include me in her work. I am always touched by this as I was just another student, but she valued me as an individual as she did all her students. During this time, I got to know Jill personally. She would begin her morning with yoga and tea, then put on her essential oils (always lavender), and end with words of affirmation. At times, I would come to her with problems, and she would take time out of her busy schedule to listen and give advice. If you knew Jill, that also meant reading was assigned that related to the issue. I am forever grateful I had this time with her. Her presence was the calming beacon I needed in my last semester. I still have several of her assigned readings saved on my flash drive that I revisit when I need a reminder of her warmth. If I had to narrow down Jill's infinite wisdom, I would say she helped me learn my worth as an individual and as a woman. I wish that Jill could have seen Greta Gerwig's *Barbie*, because I know she would have loved how it inspired women around the world.

As I reflect on Dr. Jill Eichhorn's life and legacy, I cannot help but think of the lasting kindness she spread throughout the community of Clarksville. Her leadership and positivity still radiate at Austin Peay's campus through her lasting work in the Women's and Gender Studies Department. Around the time of her passing in October 2022, many people began throwing around the term "What Would Jill Do?" I immediately latched onto this phrase. *What would Jill do?* She would treat everyone with unrelenting kindness. She would give words of encouragement freely. She would believe in every person she encountered. And you better bet she would assign a reading to help you through an issue. These are the attributes I feel embody her legacy.

I end my tribute to Jill by asking that we all work to carry on her legacy. Whether you were a colleague, student, family member, or friend, we can all look to her as an inspiration. Even if you feel your work is small, know that you are making a difference in the fight for equality. There are days when I wish I could ask her advice again, but I carry her words with me and sprinkle them into everything I do. Even though she is no longer with us, her kindness carries on in each and every one of us.

The Baby Train
Nonfiction by Bryanna Licciardi

"I'm not much of a kid person."

"Do you mean infants? Toddlers?" the therapist asked.

"All of the above?"

"I see," she said casually, writing something down in her yellow notepad, though we both knew the reaction was anything but casual. In this society, the kid question always asked shouldering the answer, because everyone wants children, even if only "someday." As a woman who has never enjoyed the company of children—who in fact has been known to hide when she hears one coming—I've found it easier to just evade questions like this with humor. However, this was a serious decision I was about to make, so I answered truthfully.

Without looking up, she said, "And I'm assuming you're not married?"

Assuming? "Yes, I'm single."

"Why do you think you're single?"

What kind of question was that? Because men suck at dating me? Because I suck at dating them? Because I've become an expert at *not* dating?

Instead, I said, "I'm a virgin. And guys tend not to know what to do with that."

Her face was priceless—mouth open, eyes crooked yet bugging. She looked stunned, like she'd just discovered the missing link. "Virgin...," she mumbled. "And you're twenty-four?"

I nodded.

She leaned forward, pen pressed hard onto her pad while she spewed out textbook clichés trying to unlock the secret: was there a history of trauma; was I controlled by the church; had I any daddy issues? But alas, as hard as it was to believe, I was a virgin simply because I'd never had sex.

The typical reaction to this news was the whole "Why are you saving yourself?" or "Why do you think you're so special?" Or my favorite, "The first time is going to be awful, so you might as well get it over with." It wasn't until I took a women's studies class in college that I found the best answer to this question: it was none of their business. That professor became my favorite for a reason.

The therapist eventually moves on. "Well, being in your...situation...as an egg donor is unusual. Do you think that would affect your inclination to meet the child?"

"I don't think so," I said, glad to finally have a question I felt comfortable answering. "I couldn't see the kid as being mine in anyway. No attachment: nothing to compel me."

"And why do you want to be a donor?"

"Have you tried being a professional student lately?" I laughed. "Graduate school is expensive. I mean, I'm glad I can help people by doing this, but honestly, I need the money."

She handed me a business card in case I ever wanted to "talk about things." I looked at it curiously during the elevator ride down. In the lobby, I threw it away in a bin outside of the building's big revolving doors.

*

After the doctors confirmed my health and sanity, the agency transferred me to a lawyer because, apparently, the legalese behind egg donation is elaborate, and I'd need representation. I scheduled an hour with him, thinking that an hour was a bit ridiculous. Until, that is, I opened the computer the next day and watched the contract download for almost twenty minutes. In it, every detail of every possible scenario was discussed: *I'd only get paid if I followed procedures exactly. If the baby came out deformed, it may or may not be as a result of my eggs. I could be investigated accordingly. Do I understand that the eggs become the parents' property, to do with as they please? Though the donation is anonymous, the child has a right to request my identity after it turns eighteen. I have a right to decline...*

Every section, subsection, and sub-subsection grew more specific. Around page thirty-eight, I finally realized how serious this was. I was giving away a key ingredient to life. I was giving them a baby, essentially. This child would have my freckles, my eyes, maybe even my cowlick. It was surreal to think of some kid growing up with my genes, never knowing that she (I'm picturing a girl) came from me. Would I ever want to meet her? Even though I have such unease around children, with their sticky fingers and lack of social skills, I thought I wouldn't mind seeing her. Maybe just in a picture, happy with her parents. That way I'd feel good about what I did. Unless she came out distorted or psychopathic. I would not take credit for a serial murderer.

Once my contract was finalized and signed, the pharmacy delivered a very expensive egg-making kit. I set alarms, placed my hormones in the fridge next to the orange juice, had my last glass of wine, and mentally prepared for what was to come.

*

Each morning, for one month, I woke at dawn to inject myself with synthetic hormones. The nurse explained that the goal of these treatments was to overstimulate my ovaries so that the lab had plenty of chances to get it right when combining eggs with the father-to-be's sperm. The nurse mentioned side effects but brushed them off as no big deal. Seeking reassurance, I scoured online forums for others who'd also taken these injections. I had a hard time finding any content written by donors and a few from women who'd taken the same medication to get pregnant: *Weight gain! Strange food cravings... Migraines... I never stopped peeing... Forget sleep!* It didn't take me long to live out their complaints for myself.

As someone who's afraid of needles, I never thought I would be capable of sticking myself with one, let alone dozens. To my surprise, I did it with little hesitation for thirty mornings and evenings in a row, barely awake. I sat on the toilet, grabbed a handful of stomach, and stabbed. Though my instinct was to get it over with quickly, fear that I'd mess up slowed me down. I'd try to go back to bed, rubbing the sore spot on my stomach, but sleep was often too far gone.

My nightly shots—the hormone stimulators—were even worse. The needle was thicker and the syringe harder to push. After a week, my stomach grew blotchy with bruises. It got harder and harder to find a spot to inject that wasn't too tender. I moved on to my thighs, but ran out of room there too.

After almost three weeks, discouragement began to tinge my thoughts. I kept trying to tell myself: *one month, one less student loan.* Because, after all, this decision to donate began with my mounting debt. They say everything in your life is there for a reason. Graduate school was making me a better (though broker) writer. What was this donation doing for me, except for sticking it to friends and family who had ever made me feel like my body wasn't my choice? I decided to call my mom for some support.

Over the phone, I whined about my bloated and bruised belly, my sporadic emotions; how I actually cried when a contestant from *The Voice* got eliminated. She paused, *hmming,* and said, "You know, if we could only get some semen in you, you'd be having triplets at least...and I'd have my grandchild quota."

*

After I started the hormones, started going to the hospital every morning for testing, I noticed my commitment deepening. I was vital to this family. My body was vital to this family, and I needed to take care of it. I read the ingredients on food boxes, avoided caffeine, and steered clear of liquor stores. I went home after class because I was too tired, called it a night when parties got too smoky. Though I never saw myself a maternal being, a bizarre relationship developed—me and my eggs. I was the mother to a tiny thing, or to several tiny things. I wasn't caressing my stomach and singing them lullabies, but I knew that my eggs needed care.

I also felt out of very place. No one else I knew was going through this. This was especially true in the fertility clinic waiting room, a place I visited all too often during my donation. Couples sporting eager faces filled the room each visit. During my first ultrasound, I sat waiting impatiently. My foot bounced so hard that my shoe fell off. I flipped through the pages of a *People* magazine that I had no interest in. The woman next to me took notice of my jitteriness.

"Your first time here?" she asked, glancing not-so-discreetly at my belly. I shrugged, smiling back, not wanting to lie but realizing she assumed I was either pregnant or trying to get there.

After a few seconds of waiting for a reply, she said, "Don't worry. You'll be fine."

I could guess what she was thinking: *How old is she? What's wrong with her? Is she like me? Where is her partner?* I didn't belong in that room with those people. When no one was looking, I slipped my silver JCPenney ring off my right hand and onto my ring finger. I held out my hand and looked at it, laughing quietly to myself. But I left it there.

When they finally called my name, I was relieved to leave the public eye. The nurse, a woman not much older than me, led me down the zigzagging hallway and into a dark room. In the middle of that room was the chair. Any woman who's gone to a gynecologist knows the chair. It's high, usually with a stool beside to help you climb, draped in thin paper, equipped with the dreaded stirrups at one end. A large machine was set up next to the chair, its screen blinking dark blue. My nurse pointed to a bathroom door on the opposite side. "You can leave your clothes in there," she said, handing me a hospital gown. "Take off everything below the waist."

I felt ridiculous climbing into the chair, paper crinkling underneath, my gown tangling and slipping open behind me. The nurse placed my feet up in the stirrups and entombed my legs with a sheet. She unsheathed the ultrasound probe from a drawer. It was a thick, long, white, rounded weapon-of-an-instrument covered in clear plastic. When the nurse handed it to me, telling me to guide it in myself, I looked at it gravely.

"No. You don't understand," I said weakly, laughing about how awkward this conversation was about to become. "This isn't going to fit. I'm still...I'm pretty much...I'm a virgin."

"Really? Well," she said, hesitating a bit. "There might be some slight tearing, but it will go in. I promise."

Liar. That's what I tried to say, but then the probe moved its first millimeter, and a scream/laugh/gargle came out of my mouth instead. I pretended it was funny because she kept laughing. I'm sure it was, to her. Especially if you ignore the blood I had to wipe from between my legs.

*

As luck would have it, the extraction surgery fell on Thanksgiving Day. The nurse called me two days prior with instructions to stop the hormones that day and details to administer one last shot. The big one. They called it the hCG, or in layman's terms, *human chorionic gonadotropin.* I looked it up, and, according to the web, its job was to force my eggs to tear from my ovary wall in preparation for surgery. Because this shot needed to go all the way into my muscles, the nurse said that the buttocks would be the best injection site, and she recommended I find someone to inject it for me. Since it was a holiday, all my roommates were leaving town, so I'd be alone the night it was needed.

One of them, who just so happened to be in a nursing program, offered to set up the syringe the day she left. When she pulled it out of its box, I almost fainted. The needle itself, not including the syringe, was the length of my hand and almost as thick as a pencil. As she mixed the medicine, she explained that since I couldn't reach my own butt, I'd have to inject this monster into the next thickest place—my thigh.

"You're pretty small," she warned. "So be really careful not to hit any bone. That could do some serious damage."

I watched my roommates leave one by one by one (I was broke, so I had a lot of roommates) and, once alone, set my alarm for 2:40 a.m. I thought it might be easier to stay up, but I didn't make it past 11. When my alarm went off, I was awake instantly. I ran to the fridge, snatched the ready-made shot, and jumped back into bed. With the lights on and my legs spread out before me, I stared at the left thigh, my chosen victim. How fragile it looked; how much it depended on me to keep it safe. Before I could chicken out, I stabbed.

After every drop had left the syringe, I slipped the needle out. When the last of it escaped my skin, a strong stream of blood followed. I hadn't prepared for that and tried to stop the bleeding with my hand while I grabbed the nearest thing, a yellow bandana, to tie around my thigh. When I woke up the next morning, I had a crusty blood and yellow tie-dye bandana tied to my leg, and a limp. My thigh was swollen and sore. I spent the day in bed, massaging it, avoiding any thoughts of my impending surgery, of what I was doing to myself.

*

I arrived at the hospital in the early afternoon on Thanksgiving, aware that families across the country were already on their second helpings of casseroles and turkey legs. The hospital was busier than I'd anticipated, and it took a while to check in. I'd only gotten a few hours of sleep, so I was tired, and luckily so. Sleepiness overrode my nerves, though the nerves built up the longer I waited.

Eventually, a nurse called Kathy led me through double doors covered in cautionary signs. "WARNING: NO PERFUMED CREAMS, LOTIONS, OR DEODORANTS BEYOND THIS POINT!" I couldn't remember if I'd put on any deodorant and discreetly sniffed my armpits.

Kathy ushered me to an empty bed and gave me a gown to change into. As she prepared the anesthesia, she asked me to hold out my arms so she could find a juicy vein and gasped at the bruises she found. "Oh, honey."

I looked down at my arms, seeing the many needle marks left behind from the countless blood tests I'd been subjected to. Her reaction startled me, and, whether from exhaustion or fear, I started shaking. She tried to get the anesthesia into place, but none of her needles found a vein. Three stabs and bloody swabs later, Kathy gave up. "You're too cold and dehydrated, and your veins are too beat up," she said, rubbing her warm hands over my cold ones. Before she left, Kathy wrapped my arms in a blanket and placed small heating pads in my hands. I was so weak I could barely hold onto them, and the weakness felt like defeat. A few minutes later, she came back with a very pale man, an anesthesiologist, who quickly slipped the needle into my forearm. He spoke with a European accent I couldn't place and told jokes without smiling as he followed Kathy and me to the operating room.

While the nurse secured my IV drip, one of the doctors helped me climb onto the operating table and flung my legs from the side of the table into very tall stirrups. I didn't think I could reach them but, somehow, I slid in my legs up to the calves. As I tried to ignore the fact that my lady parts were now very exposed,

I noticed how many people were there with me. I counted at least eight faces, half-concealed by masks, before the anesthesiologist slipped plastic around my face. This was beginning to feel like torture.

"Please put me out," I murmured to him, my voice muffled by the plastic of the anesthesia mask. There was a slight, bitter smell I recognized as the laughing gas from the dentist, but my nerves kept me alert. "I don't want to be awake for this."

"Ah," he said in his quiet accent. "Since this is your holiday, I make you a special cocktail. It tastes bad, but you will not care." In my last few seconds of consciousness, I saw the crowd of scrubs creeping in.

*

My stepmom told the rest of our family that I'd missed Thanksgiving because I had come down with something. She said she did it to keep my privacy, but I think she did it out of embarrassment.

"My family wouldn't understand," she said. "They're Catholic."

I didn't know what my eggs had to do with being Catholic, but I didn't care. It was over. My check would be in the mail Monday morning, and I had finally seen this thing through. I thought I'd feel more accomplished, more relieved. But I lay in bed for three days, bleeding and lonely. At first I thought it was because nobody could understand what I'd gone through, that I'd worked so hard for so many weeks and it was suddenly over. I later read that this is a normal reaction, that my body was just crashing from hormone withdrawal.

*

If someone asked me to describe the process of donating eggs, I'd call it awful, fascinating, transformative, hilarious, and, of course, mildly lucrative. I'd slightly wondered if my maternal instincts would emerge, but, alas, children still look cuter from way, way, *way* far away. It did make me realize that this urge to have a family is very real for other people. What I'd undergone to donate must be ten times worse for the woman on the receiving end of my eggs.

I want people to accept my choices and therefore want to accept other women's choices, even if they're different from my own. Thanks to that women's studies professor, I had the confidence to be different and use this crazy experience to reclaim my body and thus my voice.

So perhaps I'll never want to give birth. Perhaps I'll never want to raise a family. Perhaps I'll never be able to look at an egg and see a child any more than I could look at a child and see an egg. Then again, eighteen years from now, if one of my donations asks to meet me, I might be forced to change my mind.

"Baby Train" first published online in *Cleaver Magazine*, 2016. Reprinted by permission of the author.

More Will Be Revealed
A Monologue for Jill
Nonfiction by Barbara Lee Gray

For more than twenty years, Dr. Jill Eichhorn's influence has benefited many of the disciplines and demographics at Austin Peay here in Clarksville, Tennessee. It has been my privilege to participate in many of the programs she introduced to this campus such as *The Vagina Monologues* and the Clothesline Project. Off campus, Jill encouraged my participation in conferences, panels, showcases for scrapbooks, student symposiums, collaborative discussions, community outreach, and I enjoyed workshops with feminist luminaries such as Eve Ensler and Peggy McIntosh. The organizations that benefited from Jill's work include: Legal Aid of Clarksville, Sexual Assault Center, Safe House, and Centerstone, scholarships for FMLA, and groups at Fort Campbell. Then there are the students who, under Jill's leadership and coordination, formed bonds with one another, learned to support the community, and collaborated in leadership programs of their own through the Feminist Majority Leadership Alliance. This monologue is in celebration of Dr. Jill Eichhorn's legacy.

Spring of 2002:
    the Acting III professor talked about
    monologues the women in the class were going to perform.
    they invited me to visit the class,
Dr. Eichhorn's class
    (which met every year for the next twenty years)
was participating in a simultaneous,
    nation-wide performance of the play
    The Vagina Monologues
    high noon Valentines Day, V-Day.
"The Flood," assigned to me by the student director.

The next year, I was the organizer and traveled to Chicago to
bond with Eve Ensler, who taught us to bond with each other.
Spring 2002 – The Clothesline Project
Jill hung T-shirts, a clothesline strung among the few saplings
that grew in the yard in front of Harned Hall (not long after the
tornado of 1999)
Intrigued by the shirts, I read them, pinned them to the line
    before class.
There was no UC or quad or plaza;
 they were building the new one so Jill used the yard in front of
    Harned Hall.
They finished the UC; she moved the Clothesline to the plaza.
    A decade later:
a visiting representative from Clothesline Project suggested we
choose a "must include" group of shirts from the APSU collection.
We stuck tabs of masking tape on each shirt the representative
helped us choose.
At the end of the day, a fierce storm kicked in—blew rain and
debris under the UC plaza.
We scrambled to get the shirts out of the rain before they got all
wet, hundreds of them,
all sorted out by the universe herself.

The summer of 2002: Women in Spirituality class – two words:
    Yoga, chakras
    the Reiki,
    Pope Joan
    kirlian photography,
    spirit cards (when everyone was an otter)
    drum circle
    for class
    her house
        Jill's favorite chant = *the earth, the water, the fire, the air;*
    return, return, return
This is a long beginning.

As Jill used to say: "More will be revealed."
Jill had faith in me,
More than I did in myself.

my second year of teaching,
    Jill asked me if I was interested
    teaching an online Women's Studies course.
    I had just been assigned English 1020 so I declined.
    As it happens (in academia)
        someone got my 1020.
I asked around: "any APSU 1000 classes open?"
    and there were not.
Jill was in her office "is the online class still available?"

"Yes," said Jill. And more has been revealed ever since. I learned that the same issues come up year after year on end: women's place on this good earth, a dance of two steps forward and three steps back, lately. It has been an eternal grift against the people, especially women, in most all aspects of life. From the first performance of *The Vagina Monologues* in 2002 until her death in October 2022, Jill kept the world turning, the women bonding. Every semester was a new dawn on the same issues, and the undercurrent is always the same:

Women need each other, or
    society breaks us apart
    Once we are aware
        there is no time to spare
    The heart of the earth mother demands it

We work harder for less
    It's anyone's guess
    The reason for inequality
        is a weak man's frailty
    So now the world's a mess (it's up to us).

And whom do we help
    even if they don't ask,
    even if they don't care
        And would rather despair
    By putting their life on a shelf?

The Supreme Court overturned Roe vs. Wade last May and as of August 2022, abortion is illegal in the state of Tennessee. What a dangerous turn of events for women and girls. For feminist leaders in the South, this is a dangerous place to be. And when Jill Eichhorn passed away, we lost one of our steadfast leaders in the good fight against patriarchal oppression. Where do we go from here? We have the torch. More will be revealed.

Before I Was a Feminist
Poetry by Lachon Sumers

Before I was a feminist...
I was convinced that God hated women.
That Eve was truly the world's biggest villain
And Lot's wife was nothing more than Lot's wife.

I went to a church camp and they taught about the women of the
bible.
Some had names, some were unknown.
But the truth is God didn't hate women.

People with power, who are threatened by women, hate women.

At age seven...
I carried pads, tampons, liners
The whole fixing in my purse.

At age eight...
I wore heels that made me feel powerful
Dresses that flowed in the wind
Had colorful nails that glistened in the sun.

I wanted to be a woman before I knew...
That people *THINK* they hated women.

I played sports that allowed me to
Make friends.
Run free.
Feel powerful.
Embrace my girlhood.

I was a young woman.

Free from the worries.

The troubles.
To know the stares.

The very loud stares of me sitting with my legs open with skirts
and dresses.
The very loud stares of older men admiring my body.
The very loud stares of older women judging my unkempt Hair
Clothes
Shoes
Nails

The very loud stares of me being what I decided a woman should
look like.

Then I learned that God hated women.

Until I got my period.

Riddled with a terrible headache,
A stomach ache that somehow went to my legs,
That made my knees ache,
My teeth sore,
And my eyes burn
With tears.

Until I got my boobs.

Plush bags filled with fat,
Filled with the possibility of feeding an unborn child if wanted,
Big enough to leave the training bra stage,
Still small compared to the bodies around me,
Skin that brought their own barcodes.

Until I got my stretch marks.

That I thought at first made me a tiger,
Fun to touch,
Even better to hide,
Fearful of going to the pool for my peers to see,

The time I grew six inches in a summer
Or the time I once wore a size 6 but eventually became a size 12.

Until I met her.
A woman that taught me that being a woman was beautiful.
That the color purple came in multiple shades.
        MAUVE
        SOFT LILAC
        VIOLET
        INDIGO
        IRIS
        WINE
        AMETHYST
        MAGENTA

Are a few words that make me think of you.

That semester before I decided that God didn't hate women.
God loved women so much...God gave some women periods.
  God loved women so much...God gave some women boobs of all
                                                    sizes
God loved women so much...God painted some women with
marks telling the stories of how

She became.

How the woman that...breathed in air so deep that she gave life to
her baby.
How the woman that...laughed freely, strangers from afar
admired her.
How the woman that...dressed so colorfully inspired generations
to come.
How the woman that...never gave up continued to fight.
How the woman that...inspired this poem taught women after her
how to love other women.

God loved women so much.
That he placed in my life a woman of all women.
Thank you, Jill, for all that you embodied.

Thank you for teaching that feminism and womanhood is so sacred.

50

Stages
A Monologue
Nonfiction by Jordan Hoekstra

When We First Met

Young Me: (Act innocent, naïve, optimistic, and young)
My first day of college, I can remember it so well. I was so excited but very nervous and a little insecure. Even though I had some insecurities I remember thinking that I was hot stuff because I just got my belly button pierced three months prior!

I thrived in high school. I was captain of the color guard and winter guard, in the show choir, member of Tri-M and National Honor Society. I also graduated with distinguished honors.

My whole future was ahead of me, and I was anxious to get started!

Me Now:
I was walking to my very first college class, and I saw him. He was waiting by the elevator. A tall, built, dirty-blonde hair, blue-eyed man. What I did not know that this man would turn into the person I feared the most.

Young Me: (Act innocent, naïve, optimistic, and young)
I remember thinking to myself, "Wow, this guy is cute! Ok, Jordan, just press the elevator button and ACT COOL!"

Me Now:
I noticed while we were waiting on the elevator that he started to sing out loud. He was not humming or whistling, but singing *(Pause)* out loud. I couldn't help but giggle, and that caught his attention and he started to talk to me.

Young Me: (Act innocent, naïve, optimistic, and young)

"Omg, he is talking to me!"

Me Now:

I asked what floor he was going to and he said, "Floor 2, room 210."

Young Me: (Act innocent, naïve, optimistic, and young)

Crap! We are in the same class? Ok, how in the hell am I supposed to act cool throughout this whole class period?"

Me Now:

He sat next to me in the class, passed me notes, and we even had lunch together after. He was very charming and funny. He wanted to continue to hang out that day, but I had to go to practice.

Well, after practice guess who was waiting on me? Yep, you guessed it! He then walked me to my building and even helped me carry my equipment.

As our relationship progressed, he confided in me with all of his secrets and everything that pained him. He made me feel that only I could help him and that he trusted me, and I felt that I could trust him.

There were no signs of anger or violence in the very beginning.

Young Me: (Act innocent, naïve, optimistic, and young)

I have never had someone beg for my attention before. This was nice. He made me feel like I was someone special. I remember thinking that he is a good-looking football player, so if I'm the girl by his side, and that means that I'm important, too, right?

Me Now: (Look at Young Jordan like she is crazy and shake your head)

What I didn't know was this was one of the first steps into my abusive relationship. He gave me the illusion that he idolized me and I was the dominant one in this relationship.

<u>Accused Me of Cheating</u>

Young Me: (Act hurt and as if you are questioning your self-worth)

A few months into our relationship, he accused me of cheating on him. He started to pee blood, and he accused me of giving him a sexually transmitted disease. He came to my house and cussed me out in my front yard. He called me every name you can think of. His favorite name for me was slut, all because he was not the first person I was with and that is a WHOLE other story.

Me Now:

That was his way of breaking down my confidence, making me feel bad about myself, and feel worthless. It was also a way for him to make me feel like he was superior to me, even though he was not a virgin when we met either. Double standards, don't ya think?

Young Me: (Act hurt and as if you are questioning your self-worth)

You can ask any of my family, friends, or even my ex-boyfriends, I am probably was one of the most loyal and faithful persons you will meet. I was heartbroken. I couldn't believe he thought that I could do something like that.

Me Now:

My dad and grandma could hear everything from inside the house. They did not like him from that moment on and forbid me to see him. Well, me being the love struck new "adult" that I was, I couldn't have that. So, I left home to be with him.

This was the next step into my abusive relationship-isolation, from my friends and family.

By the way, he later found out that he did not have an STD.

Young Me: (Act hurt and as if you are questioning your self-worth)

After I left home, we lived with his mom, a friend of his sister's, and even my mom's house until he pulled a knife on me in her kitchen. I don't think my mom knew about that part; she just heard us arguing in the middle of the night. My mom said he had to go. I couldn't leave him. I was terrified. I left home, burned the bridge with my father who has always been my rock, and I was too ashamed and scared to ask to go back. All I knew is that I couldn't go home and that I was scared and that I loved him.

Me Now:

I was wrapped in some fantasy world. I had no idea that I was already in an abusive relationship, at 18 years old. Later on, my mom tried to give me packets and printed off materials that explained different forms of abuse. I threw them away, wouldn't even look at them.

What is crazy is that my family liked him in the beginning. My dad made a dinner for him on his birthday, and they went to a hockey game. My mom invited him to Thanksgiving and her home. By the next Thanksgiving, everyone saw his true colors, and my mom and aunts had a little bit of fun. They offered to make his plate for him and, let's just say, they tampered with it. It was hilarious, especially after he mentioned how great the corn tasted!

I think everyone liked him in the beginning because he was a GREAT actor! He was an even better manipulator. There were times where he was yelling at me, cussing me, threatening me, or even had his hands around my neck. When someone would walk in the room, he would slap on that smile of his and act like everything was great. If they asked why I looked upset, he would tell them that I was just PMSing or being emotional. He was great at manipulating people, especially when it came to me and his family and friends.

I didn't believe that I was in an abusive relationship. When we would have an argument, he would apologize and be very loving, like he was in the beginning. Things may be good for a while, but he would go back to that man with all the rage in his eyes that I feared. I will never forget that rage in his eyes.

Valentine's Day

Young Me:

He never did anything nice on Valentine's Day. I do not care much about the material things. Of course, it is nice when someone buys you a gift, but I would have been happy with a simple dinner at home and watching movies. But, he wouldn't even acknowledge Valentine's Day. The last year I was with him, he bought me flowers, a stuffed animal, and a five-pound chocolate heart. That meant so much to me.

Me Now:

Later, he told me that the only reason why he bought me that stuff is because we thought I had cancer. We were waiting for biopsy results. Thankfully I did not have cancer, and I just had to have a small surgery. That shows the high he would put me on and then knock me straight back down.

Abuse on Campus

Young Me:

I remember one night we had nowhere to go and slept in his car on campus. You know, in that parking lot behind that baseball field? He got mad at something, I don't even remember what it was, and told me to get out of the car. It was in the middle of winter so, of course, I refused. He then got out of the car, came around to my side, pulled me out, and pushed me to the ground. I got up and started to run away. He chased me. Once he got ahold of me, he pushed me down to the ground again, pulled my hair to make me stand back up, and then pushed me down again. Someone called campus police that night. I have no idea who, but when they arrived, I told them everything was okay.

Me Now:

(*Act frustrated*) OMG! I want to kick my 18-year-old ass!!! Everything was not okay!!!

(*Act angry*) Just to give you a visual, when I met him, I was 130 pounds. At this point, four months later, I was 97 pounds from all the stress and worry. So, I'm sure you can imagine how easy it was for a 6'2", 240-pound *(do the quotation marks)* "man" to throw me around. I'm sure I looked like a rag doll being tossed around.

Oh, and this was not the only time he abused me on *(Point down and look in the audience and pause)* THIS campus. *(Point in Drane Street's direction)* You know that BCM building on Drane Street? He banged my head against that AC unit.

(Pause and take a breath like you are calming down)

We finally got a place of our own. I was hoping things would settle down, become for stable for us, and the stress would go away. But it didn't. The abuse only got worse.

<u>Driving</u>

Young Me:
For most of our relationship, I was the only one working. Yet I was still expected to clean and cook while he did nothing all day but play video games. I did not have a license, so his ONLY responsibility was to take me to work, pick me up, and to take me to Walmart when we needed groceries. He hated to take me to Walmart. He gave me a time limit, which was always unrealistic, and if I wasn't back in time, he would leave me. I always felt that I was on that game show *Super Market Sweep* anytime I had to get groceries.

He would drive erratically almost every day. He would cut in between cars and squeeze his way through, pass cars on the shoulder, drive really close to semis and then cut them off. He would wait to the last minute to brake, he would make the tires screech when he would take off, and he would go about 60-65 mph on roads where the speed limit was supposed to be 30 or 35. The worst was the road we lived on, which was 35 mph. Our road was hilly, and there was a huge curve with a drop-off. He loved scaring me on that one, and I still have issues to this day with driving and being in cars with people unless they drive like a grandma.

Me Now:
Well, not all grandmas. Mine had a lead foot.

Control

Young Me:
He loved control. He controlled who I talked to and what I wore. If I wore makeup or looked nice—I was cheating. He wanted access to my phone, emails, and social media. He also liked to control what I did at home. If he thought the bathroom needed to be cleaned, I had to clean it then. If he wanted something to eat, I had to drop everything and make him something to eat. This included if I was sleeping.

One night he got pissed at a video game. He needed to feel manly, I guess, and needed someone to control. So, he decided to wake me up so I could make him something to eat. When I refused, he took all of the covers off the bed and turned the AC unit on, which was over our bed. He then said, "Fine, you stupid bitch. I hope you freeze, you fuckin' cunt."

I hated that Xbox. He loved to play *Call of Duty*, especially at wee hours of the night. I remember waking up to him yelling, "You damn noob!" or "I pwanged you," which ironically meant owned. He was always really loud; he didn't even try to be quiet, even though I had to be up early to go to work in the morning so our bills would be paid.

Me Now:
Thankfully, his precious Xbox got the red ring of death! Bahahaha!

Forcing Himself on Me

Young Me:
He even tried to control me when it came to sex. He tried to force himself on me one day. By this time, I was disgusted by the thought of sleeping with him.

Me Now: (Supposed to be funny)

And I promise it had nothing to do with his "less than average" equipment.

Young Me:

I fought it, and I fought it, and he finally gave up.

Me Now:

What he did next shocked me and terrified me at the same time. He got off me, stood over me, and banged his hands on his chest like an ape.

His Wrist

Young Me (Act scared, apprehensive, but hopeful):

One of the times when I tried to leave him, the next morning I received a picture message on my phone of his bleeding wrist. He was put into a mental institution that day, when he was diagnosed bipolar and manic depressive. I went back to him. He needed me. I thought it all made sense. Now, it was his illness that made him do all of those mean things. He was given free medication and counseling. I was sure that we could work through this and we could have the life I dreamt of.

Me Now:

That didn't happen, he stopped taking the medication and stopped going to counseling. He didn't want to get better. I kept giving him excuses and tried to put myself in his shoes. That didn't help anything. That is why to this day, I do not like to give him excuses. I know eventually I will have to look at the facts on why he is the way he is. Was he beaten as a child, raped, or molested? Was he bullied or always put down? Or maybe it was just his mental illness. Even if he was raped, or beaten, or molested, that did not give him the right to abuse me.

There is a cycle to abuse that all of us need to understand. Not only can this behavior be taught in our homes, it can also be taught in the media and our society. Today, we live in a society in which a woman is slapped, and that is normal. If a woman is pushed, that is normal. If a man forces his wife to sleep with him, that is normal. If a man yells or puts down a woman, that is normal. Not to mention, most books shows or movies have rape scenes now. It is normalized. All of these are NOT normal, and they are not okay.

Possible Pregnancy

Young Me:

I was late on my period by a week. I was terrified to tell him that I could be pregnant. I told him that I was late while I was in the bathroom. He was furious. He said that if I was pregnant, I was getting an abortion. I refused to have one. When I told him that, he punched me in my stomach. He said, "I will take care of it then." I remember immediately falling onto the bathroom floor in the fetal position, protecting my stomach so he couldn't get to it. Other than that, I do not remember what happened.

Me Now:

When it comes to your own mortality, sometimes you disconnect yourself from what is happening to you. This happened to me, a lot. There is so much that I do not remember, and I'm thankful for that.

I know there was a struggle that day because of the condition of the bathroom afterword. The bathroom looked like a tornado hit it. The trash can was knocked over, the shower curtain was ripped and torn down, shampoo bottles were lying at the bottom of the tub, the hand towel rack was pulled out of the wall, and there was a hole in the bathroom door.

Thankfully, I was not pregnant and never was. Just because I personally wouldn't go through with an abortion does not mean that I don't think women should have the choice. You never know what kind of situation they are in. In my case, my life was threatened if I did not have one. That is why I do not feel like I have a say in what someone else does with their body.

I wish I would tell you this was the worst of it. But it only gets worse.

My Neck

Young Me:

One day I found out that he was sleeping with a girl that I worked with. When I asked him about it, things escalated quickly. Once again, there is a gap in my memory, but the next thing I remember was both of us outside in our yard. His hands were around my neck, and he was telling me to get on my knees and give him head. When I said no, he spit on my face and pushed my neck far back, my neck popped all the way down.

Me Now:

I still have problems with my neck, but at least I can say it wasn't from that. *(Look at the audience like—"y'all know what I'm talking about" — supposed to be funny)*

<u>Shower</u>

Young Me:

I was taking a shower one day, and he came into the bathroom and asked me to make him something to eat. I told him I would as soon as I got out of the shower. He said no, he wanted it now. I told him I was almost done, I just had to wash off my body. He pulled the shower curtain back, grabbed my arm, and he said, "Well I'm throwing your naked ass outside then." I tried to pull away while he was pulling me through the house, but I couldn't get away.

We got to the living room, and I dropped to the floor, hoping that would slow the process down and make him struggle. He lost his grip, and I ran into the kitchen. He came after me and grabbed my left hand. I was able to reach for a knife with my right hand that was in the dish dryer. I turned toward him and pointed it at him. He still had ahold of my left hand. He looked at me like "Really? What in the hell are you going to do with that?" He was right. What was I going to do with a knife? Knowing him, his mom, and their manipulative ways, I would be the one in jail even though it would have been in self-defense. I cannot let him ruin my life. He then began to pull me toward the door. I raised the knife up, but nothing was felt. I did it again. His eyes got big, and the next thing I see is blood.

Me Now:

I did not cut him. That day I cut myself. He knew I did not have it in me to hurt him, so he wasn't afraid. But there was a shock factor, and that interrupted his rage and he let go of me. After a few seconds of silence, he looked at me and said, "What the fuck did you do?" he pushed me to the floor and threw a dirty kitchen towel at me and said, "Here, you stupid bitch." That day, I did not cut myself to hurt myself. I wanted to live. I felt that was my only escape in that situation. From that moment on, I knew if didn't get out, one of us was could end up dead.

The Roommate

Young Me:

We lived in a duplex. He befriended the couple next door. Apparently, they were in a similar relationship. He invited the male to live with us. We only had a one bedroom, one bathroom apartment, and you had to go through our bedroom to get to the bathroom. The guy ended up sleeping on our couch for months. One night when my ex was out, I woke up with our roommate jacking off over me. I felt exposed even though I was fully clothed. I was terrified. When

Me Now:

I told him what happened. He didn't believe me. The roommate ended up staying.

My Light Bulb Moment

Young Me:

We took in a stray cat. She was wounded, and we tried to take her to Cats R Us but they were full. So, they gave us everything we needed to take care of her. We named her Buttercup. Well, we didn't know that Buttercup was pregnant! On April Fool's Day, she had two babies, Lotus and Lily. For some reason Buttercup was not producing milk, so I had to feed them this special formula twice a day. They were absolutely precious, and I became attached pretty quickly. He knew how much I loved them. So, what does he do? Threaten me with them any chance he got. When I was at work, he would call me or text me saying he was going to throw them out. Or kill them. Every day I was a nervous wreck.

One day, when I was at home, he got pissed and threw a glass in their direction, and it shattered everywhere, including on top of them. *(Stick out your hand and cup it to give a visual)* They were just a month old; they could fit in the palm of your hand.

Me Now:

I had a light bulb moment then, and it became very clear to me. What if that was my child and they saw that or were hurt by that? I did not want him to be the father of my children. I knew from that moment on, I was ready to leave for GOOD.

Packing

Young Me (Act stronger and that you have more confidence):

I started to take anything that had value or meant something to me out of the house and into our storage outside.

He would ask what I was doing, and I would tell him I'm reorganizing. He believed it because I am an organization freak! His dumbass had no idea I was getting things in order to leave him. Whenever I had a good amount ready to go, and he was not at the house, I would call my grandma and she would come to my house so I could load up her car and she would take it back to the house for my dad to unload. We finally set a date for me to leave. I was terrified. He always said that he would kill anyone that would help me leave and always told me that if I left, he would come at me when I least expect it.

Me Now:

He got a message from his cousin wanting him to come to a family reunion in Maryland. His aunt and cousin paid for a bus ticket for him to get there. I had a free pass! This is when I knew it was meant to be, and God was looking over me and my family. I was able to move out safely with the remainder of my stuff and my three precious babies. I was able to get the process started for an order of protection before he even came home. I left him the summer of 2009. I was in this abusive relationship for three years, and I consider myself lucky. Many women are not lucky enough to get out that quick.

<u>Closing</u>

Young Me:

A lot of people wonder or ask, 'why don't the women in abusive relationships just leave?' That is honestly one of the most offensive things you can ask an abused woman. It is like you are saying it is our fault that we stayed in the relationship, like we wanted it, and that it is easy to leave. I can promise you that is not the case. He threatened the lives of my mom's side of the family, he threatened my dad's life, my life, my cat's life, and threatened to slit my grandma's throat. It is extremely dangerous to leave. When you leave, that means they have lost their power and control over you, and that pisses them off more than anything. Statistics show that when women leave their abusers, that is when most deaths occur.

Even though I left him in 2009, I was still in denial. The fear came back full force in December of 2012, when the Sandy Hook school shooting happened. I remember thinking, *who* could do such a *thing?* He came to my mind. If he was having one of his episodes, I could see him going off the deep end and doing something monstrous. I came out of denial when I took my first Women and Gender Studies course that next month. That course opened up my eyes and showed me just how bad of a situation I was actually in. I try to downplay it because I know that many other women that have had it way worse than me and have lost their lives. I had to realize that everyone's story is different, and that doesn't mean that mine was any less painful.

Me Now:

Unfortunately, I hate to admit it, but he still has some control over me. If I am riding with someone and they go too fast around curves or hug them, I feel like I am in that car with him. When I hear of women that were in abusive relationships that didn't make it, I go back to those times where that could have been me. If he would have driven a little faster, choked or smothered me a little longer, banged my head a little harder, or if he would have used that knife on me in my mother's kitchen that night, I may not be here today. My parents may have lost their daughter.

Those words he spoke, "I will come at you when you least expect it." I still hear that often in my head. I believed him when he said it, and I still do. I honestly feel that when things go wrong for him and he is having one of his episodes, he will come after me. But I cannot think that way. I am a different person than I was. I am stronger. I am fierce. I am thankful that I am here. Yes, I have the physical scars, and an indention on my upper lip from him throwing a remote control at my face, but I am alive.

So, I am here now to tell my story and hopefully touch someone that may be in an abusive relationship, know of someone that is, or is a survivor themselves. Anyone can find themselves in this type of relationship. I was a confident, kind, smart young woman. And I ended up in this type of relationship. It is a vicious cycle. My grandmothers, mom, aunts, great aunts, and my father have all been abused in some form or another. This monologue is for them and myself. This cycle stops with me. My children will not be added to this list of people that have been abused in my family.

I often beat myself up for dating him. I could already have my bachelor's degree, be living on my own, or have a husband and children. I have to remind myself that it is okay, everyone has their own journey. If it were not for this relationship, I would not be the person that I am now. I am not giving him credit for where I am in life. He is the abuser. I am giving myself credit for the struggles I have had to overcome and the work I have had to do to be the person I am now—the survivor! I am so proud of that person. Now, I have graduated college, found my precious husband, and we have two beautiful boys. I'm blessed. Our life is blessed.

A Float for Jill
Tanka by Shana Thornton

65

Canoes glide through suns
reflecting on the river's
collage of bright leaves
the bald eagle breaks away
shadows and stares as we pass.

The Vagina Quilt
Collaborative Artwork
About the Artwork by Cynthia Marsh

The 2009/2010 *The Vagina Monologues* class collaborated with the Goldsmith Press & Rare Type Collection to create *The Vagina Quilt*. The Vagina Quilt Project was conceived and created by professors Jill Eichhorn, Lee Gray, and Cynthia Marsh. Members of the class typeset and printed fabric squares that addressed or described their vaginas. The finished *Vagina Quilt* served as a backdrop for the annual *Vagina Monologues* performance on the campus of APSU.

Tribute
Nonfiction by Shauna Snyder

Dr. Eichhorn taught *The Vagina Monologues* at APSU. That year, 2010, we made a quilt together, and I got to spend so much extra time with her after school helping to screen print the pieces. I very much enjoyed this project and getting to know her more. Making this quilt, each person got to design their own square and what we wanted it to say. Mine was about taking back the silence that I experienced from an abusive childhood. I found this experience to be profoundly empowering. I still am close to many of the people I had this class with, even though it was many years ago. I never forgot her gentle way of challenging people into a higher level of thinking. It was so thoughtful and kind. She was resilient and strong. She validated feelings and was not afraid of difficult or uncomfortable conversations. I could never fully put into words how much she meant to me and how she shaped my life thereafter. I believe the seeds she planted in me and so many others have forever changed the landscape of our community at large. I hope to continue her legacy in my life as I remember the way she has shaped my life and continue to look within and gently challenge my uncomfortable and difficult feelings. I will always try to be a better person due to her lifelong example of her life and work. I am forever inspired by her influence.

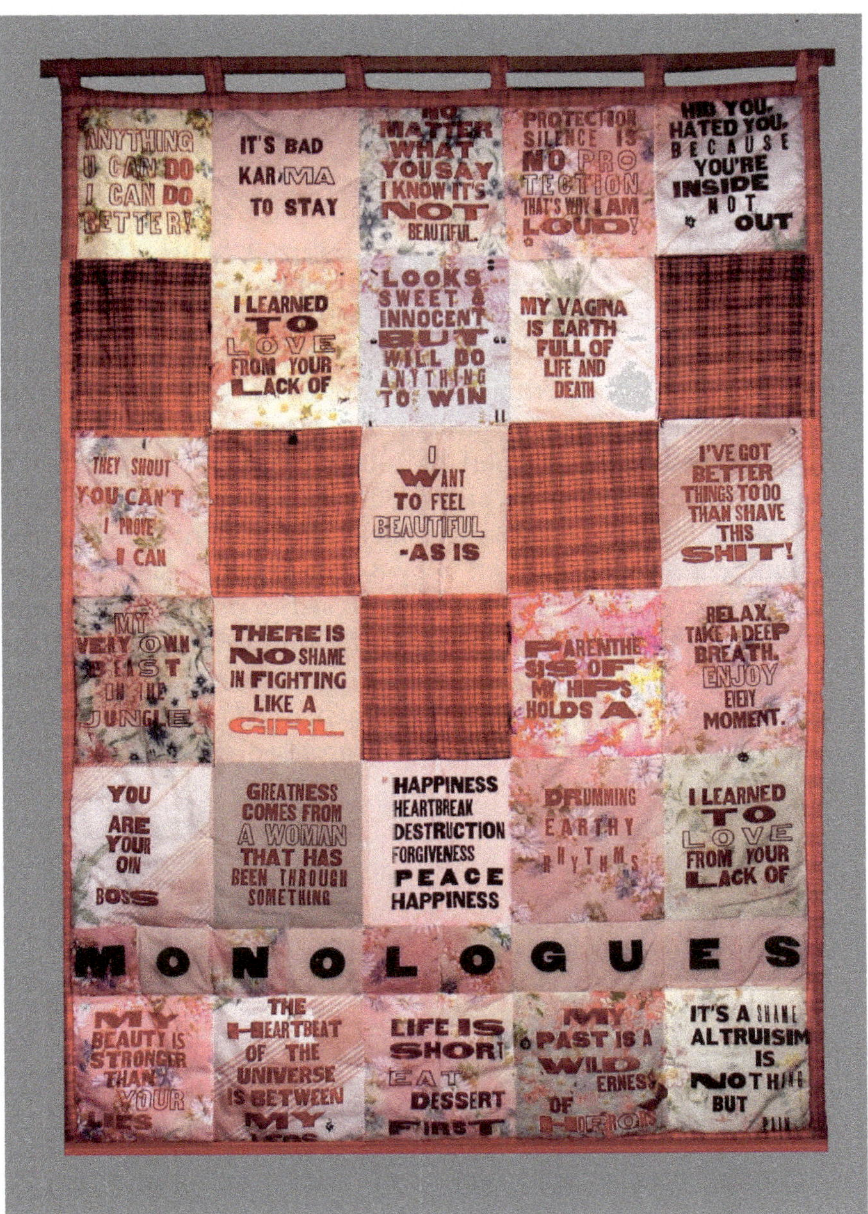
ANYTHING U CAN DO I CAN DO BETTER!
IT'S BAD KARMA TO STAY
NO MATTER WHAT YOU SAY I KNOW IT'S NOT BEAUTIFUL.
PROTECTION SILENCE IS NO PROTECTION THAT'S WHY I AM LOUD!
HID YOU, HATED YOU, BECAUSE YOU'RE INSIDE NOT OUT
I LEARNED TO LOVE FROM YOUR LACK OF
Looks SWEET & INNOCENT -BUT- WILL DO ANYTHING TO WIN
MY VAGINA IS EARTH FULL OF LIFE AND DEATH
THEY SHOUT YOU CAN'T I PROVE I CAN
I WANT TO FEEL BEAUTIFUL -AS IS
I'VE GOT BETTER THINGS TO DO THAN SHAVE THIS SHIT!
MY VERY OWN BEAST IN THE JUNGLE
THERE IS NO SHAME IN FIGHTING LIKE A GIRL
PARENTHESIS OF MY HIPS HOLDS A
RELAX, TAKE A DEEP BREATH, ENJOY EVERY MOMENT.
YOU ARE YOUR OWN BOSS
GREATNESS COMES FROM A WOMAN THAT HAS BEEN THROUGH SOMETHING
HAPPINESS HEARTBREAK DESTRUCTION FORGIVENESS PEACE HAPPINESS
DRUMMING EARTHY RHYTHMS
I LEARNED TO LOVE FROM YOUR LACK OF
MONOLOGUES
MY BEAUTY IS STRONGER THAN YOUR LIES
THE HEARTBEAT OF THE UNIVERSE IS BETWEEN MY LEGS
LIFE IS SHORT EAT DESSERT FIRST
MY PAST IS A WILD ERNESS OF HORROR
IT'S A SHAME ALTRUISIM IS NOTHING BUT

The Knitting Quilt
Collaborative Artwork
About the Artwork by Cynthia Marsh

The Knitting Quilt (2008) was a collaborative work produced by the students in the Women in Art class—an APSU 2008 spring semester course offering. This interdisciplinary class, taught by professors Jill Eichhorn and Cynthia Marsh, focused on the study of literary and visual art produced by women from a variety of cultural, geographic, ethnic, and historic backgrounds. Students were required to create works of art inspired by some of the historic and cultural periods studied. After a discussion concerning the domestic arts produced by women during the American Revolution, class members were taught to knit. The assignment was to knit an 8-by-8-inch square using recycled fibers or materials. Some students refused to do the assignment: they felt the requirement (learning to knit, etc.) supported the ongoing subjugation and exploitation of women. These students were asked to write and print statements in protest of knitting. The completed squares and words of protest were combined into a free-form quilt or afghan.

WHICH WAY DOES IT GO?
CASTING ON, CASTING OFF...
TWISTED YARN & NOTHING MORE...
THESE INTRICATE MOVES WEAVE IN & OUT
TWISTING TOGETHER TO FORM A SQUARE.
I was sitting in my rocking chair
KNITTING YOU A QUILT
and then I realized something...
I FEEL THE EMPTINESS
I HATE KNITTING
WHY SHOULD I DO IT?
EACH ROW REPRESENTS TIME
I COULD BE SPENDING TIME ON MYSELF
A MOMENT TO SPARE
IS ALL I'VE EVER WANTED
AFTER AWHILE I ATTEMPT AGAIN
THEN A COUPLE (7) SWIGS OF GIN
COULDN'T GET THE LOOP OF IT THO'
TO BUY YARN I WILL NEVER GO.
NEEDLES
YARN
In the past, great women have knit beautiful things.
HOW CAN I
COMPARE?
NOW KNITTING IS A MAN'S WORLD
MANUFACTURED WITHOUT CARE.
EACH STITCH A WORK OF MACHINE HANDS.
THE FABRIC OF THIS NATION IS NO
LONGER SEWN TOGETHER TIRELESSLY
BY MOTHERS, GRANDMOTHERS, SISTERS
KNITTING. AND THE LESS CARE PUT INTO A
GARMENT, THE SOONER IT WILL FALL APART.
WHO AM I?
WHAT CAN I DO?
I CLOTHE THE WORLD-
CURSED FOR THE LIFE I CAN
GIVE WITH YARN & NEEDLES
WE ARE MODERN WOMEN
WE PAY HOMAGE TO THOSE BEFORE US
SOME OF US KNITTED OUR RESPECT
& SOME SHOW RESPECT BY REVOLTING

Jill
WoodArt and poetry by Beatrix Brockman

I have no words
I pour my grief into this purple wood

Eyes on the lines the blade is cutting
Mind wrapped around the you that was

Walnut curves the arms and shoulders
Wenge goes where eyes don't see.

With care I choose the grain
Observe direction
Just as I choose the words I speak.

Bloodwood is the figure's heart,
between the chevron of the vest

With you I could be me
With you I dropped my masks

I have no words
Instead I made a pattern
Cut wood for all to see:

This is
My tribute
Jill

I have no words
I poured my grief and thoughts
into this Purple Heart

Two Haiku for Jill
Poetry by Terry Morris

Melody missed notes
Long for accompaniment—
Together we sing.

Breath of a woman.
Push for the magic of birth.
Vaginas exhale.

Untitled
Artwork and Nonfiction by Daniel Christian

The spirit of life expressed through creation of music, harmony, connection, patience, kindness, love, sincerity, generosity, excitement, and tenderness.

Jill was a person of possibility. She saw the good in the journey that each of us can undertake to improve each moment of our life, our community, and our world.

Always of the new day, Jill saw the sun rise in each of us anew and reached out to connect and find the breath of release with us. Our peace.

Jill saw her music as a child to tenderly nurture. Ever thoughtful of the process, kind to listen and receive the teachings of others, incorporating gentle balance into her wisdom, Jill's work flows through kind word and deed, spreading her vision of unity.

We breathe. We pause. We breathe. We open the channels and weave together an existence of love. Healing. We breathe. Tiny light, O great shining light.

Forever, the light in Jill shines through the light of me and through us all.

Representation
Nonfiction by Tracy Jepson

Growing up in a world of indoctrinated Baptists, I had no memory of a woman like Jill. I was taught women were "the weaker vessel" and that God intended for men to be our authority. I was taught that my opinions could not be trusted because I am female, and that I was more emotional or even hysterical if I dared express them.

I was taught my body did not belong to me, and that I should "let God decide" how many babies I had.

I had finally and painfully separated myself from that world, feeling with certainty that there would be nothing left of me if I stayed. That my spirit would die beneath the dark burden that generations of patriarchy and shame placed upon me.

Then one day I daringly (for me) walked into a Unitarian Universalist church in Clarksville, Tennessee. Of course, Jill was there, helping to nurture a community of freethinkers and outliers within the Bible belt.

"Who is this person?" I thought.

I noticed she did not dress or style her hair according to gender stereotypes.

I noticed she was educated, accomplished, and confident.

I noticed she considered herself equal in her marriage and in her profession.

I noticed that she celebrated being a mother, but she had chosen that role freely and on her own terms.

She was a woman from an older generation than I—one of the women who paved the way for the rest of us to dare to be equal. She led the way, and she bore the brunt. She was one of those rarities that later would become common. One of the first blooms on a beautiful hill that would later display many, many flowers.

But she was new to me then. I had never seen *her* type of woman before.

Representation is so important.

How many women did she give this gift to throughout her life? The gift of example.

I began thinking about this gift more deeply after her passing. And how many women younger than I had almost become unaware of it.

But not anymore.

The ground that was gained is being challenged, and now we must call upon the essence of women like Jill to strengthen us and to renew our determination.

As for me, I am the first woman in my lineage to self-actualize, to be equal in relationship, to achieve an education according to my aptitude, and to embody my full self within my community. I understand what this means, and how it feels. I will not be going back.

I often think about a quote from my favorite author, Sue Monk Kidd*, and how it applies to women like Jill. I even put it on my fridge to remind me of its directive daily. It speaks to something deep down in my being.

She says, "There is no place so awake and alive as the edge of becoming. More than that, birthing the kind of woman who can authentically say, 'My soul is my own' and then embody it in her life, her spirituality, and her community is worth the risk and hardship." I learned to live that. I learned to push through the layers of dogma and expectations that had buried me beneath them and to emerge. And I will always be thankful to Jill and women like her, for showing us what that looks like and that indeed, yes, it can be done! That we can grow to be our full selves without apology.

Jill Eichhorn was a woman in full bloom.

*Sue Monk Kidd quotation from *The Dance of the Dissident Daughter* (Harper Collins, 2016).

Instructions for How to Survive a Nuke
Poetry by Bryanna Licciardi

77

Here is where I grab your hand to pretend things work out.

Can you take a seat? Give you a minute. Let you process.
You ask me what happens next. Knowing nothing else,
I shrug. Our hands are still supposed to be touching.

Can you take a seat? Give you a minute. Let you process.
My voice tries to sound soothing as my face tries to give me away.
I shrug. Our hands are still supposed to be touching.
What comes next will feel like an ending. But for now,

here is where I grab your hand

Jill Showed Up
Poetry by Beverly Fisher

When a gathering needed an enthusiastic audience,
Jill showed up with her hearty laugh.

When the Friends of Dunbar Cave needed a guide through the
cave for a fundraising event,
Jill showed up.

When medical emergencies arose,
Jill showed up (once, twice, thrice)
to comfort and give wise counsel.

When her seven-year-old daughter lost a floatie on the river,
Jill showed up, swimming
toward the dangerous strainer to retrieve it
and saving her determined daughter
who wanted to save it herself.

When the Bread and Words event
at Austin Peay State University needed food donations,
Jill showed up with pumpkin soup.

When the odd and the quirky needed non-judgmental
acceptance, love and yes, celebration,
Jill showed up.

When Red River Breeze was onstage
performing their Celtic/Renaissance/Old-Time/World music,
Jill showed up with her recorder
that she started learning at age fifty-eight.

When another birthday rolled around,
Jill, her recorder and the gift of her songs showed up
to make it seem like your birth was the most magical event

the world had ever witnessed.

When the Unitarian Universalist Fellowship needed to begin
and continue,
Jill showed up with her time, her recorder, her donations,
her glowing presence and her three-bean casserole.

When the women (and men!) of college-age, (or any age!)
needed enlightenment and gentle guidance,
Jill showed up.

When a trail wanted to be walked, a river called for the kayaks,
when a child searched for a beacon,
when a student yearned for inspiration,
when a vagina needed a monologue,
when an event summoned hummus,
Jill showed up.

As shown by the thoughtful former students on the hospital staff
that came to her bed as she lay dying,
Jill's full and loving life still shows
in the actions, memories, words and hearts
of her husband, her children, numerous students, admiring
colleagues, and countless friends.

Jill showed up. Jill was there.

And she is still there... and here... in our broken, but grateful
hearts.

Epitome of Grace
Nonfiction by Jordan Hoekstra

It is quite ironic how Jill and I crossed paths. Straight out of high school, I was in a very abusive relationship. However, within that horrendous relationship, there was a gem to be found, my ex's sister: we kept in touch after I left that abusive relationship. She invited me out one night to see a play called *The Vagina Monologues*, and hesitantly I went. Three beautiful ladies on stage performed this play. One of them was an older lady, and part of her script was to say the F word. It cracked me up to see this older lady cussing like that. And of course, for those that have seen the play, the 'climax' was even more hilarious to see her perform. I just had to know who this lady was, so I picked up my program and saw "Dr. Jill Eichhorn, Women's and Gender Studies Department, APSU." At that point in my life, I was unsure of what direction I wanted to go in for my education, so I was curious about what this Women's and Gender Studies Department was all about.

WGS was a whole new world, something I never experienced. Jill cultivated a warm place for learning, healing, and growing and a safe place to tell your story. You were met with compassion and grace. When I started taking classes in the WGS department, I was a shell of a human being. I was just making it day by day, all of my trauma I had buried deep, I was numb for the most part. On my very first day, it was like a lid was blown off, waves of emotion consumed me, and I had no idea how to manage it. Luckily, I was in the right place.

Through these classes, I have met the most incredible people. People that were abused sexually, physically, mentally, emotionally, and economically; these people were like me. We all had different stories, but we all actively listened to each other. We supported one another. We built each other up. I had never experienced such close-knit relationships before, and it was beautiful. Most of us have gone our own ways, but I know the love still between us is just as strong. Jill taught us about community, awareness, self-care, advocacy, and leadership through our coursework and our student organization, FMLA. She taught us to use our voices and that our experiences and stories can help others.

I know this sounds cliché, but I would not be where I am today if it were not for Jill. Not only did I meet my two best friends through her classes, and one of them reintroduced me to my now husband whom I share two beautiful boys with, but she also helped me find myself. She helped me find the person I once was before all the trauma; she helped me make that person even stronger, softer, more open-minded, and fiercer. Jill guided me to do things that I never thought I would do. Public speaking is a big one. I performed in many shows of *The Vagina Monologues* at APSU, and I spoke on several panels for conferences/events. She also got me to write! I am horrible at grammar, but she strongly urged me to write. I ended up writing a monologue of my story, which was performed several times at APSU. After reading it, she told me I should write a book. I laughed at her and said, "Jill, you know my grammar!" and then said with a big smile and laugh, "That's what editors are for." I also wrote for the Feminist Majority Foundation before graduating from college. There was just something about Jill that made you feel that you could do anything!

This is just what Jill meant to me, what she did for my life. Can you imagine how many lives she has changed throughout her life and career? Family, friends, APSU, alums, myself, and the world will not be the same without Jill.

There are so many things that I will miss about Jill; her knowledge, perspective, compassion, voice, grace, sense of ease, experiences, and hummus! Lol.

Thank you, Jill, for being such an incredible human being. I love you.

Jill Saw Me
Poetry by Valerie Guzman

Jill Eichhorn—a woman who impacted the lives of others
and who knew no bounds.
Jill's profound love for women
and her unwavering belief in their worth
were the guiding forces behind her journey.
She had a rare ability to see beyond the surface
and recognize the inherent beauty and strength potential
in each individual she encountered.
Jill saw me.

Jill's remarkable capacity for empathy
created a safe space for women
to be heard, seen, and valued.
She possessed a unique ability to understand
the struggles and challenges they faced,
fostering an environment of support and empowerment.
Her genuine compassion and unwavering dedication
touched the lives of countless women,
providing them with the strength to embrace
their true selves
and fulfill their dreams.
Jill saw me, Valerie Guzman.

Best Gift
Nonfiction by Amy Wright

Before practice begins in the quiet of a yoga room, mats unroll like waves lapping a shoreline. Bare toes print the glossy hardwood as body after body settles onto the sand of the mind. This seascape remains incomplete, though, until The Yogi with the Ocean Breath exhales her first dappled deep-drawn lungful. It sounds like the crest of a heart spilling over. Awash with awareness, the studio becomes a cove.

What it means to hold space for someone, I learned from her.

How many people do you get to meet in a lifetime who can sanctify a room by breathing? People often say of certain men that they have a "commanding presence." Jill's presence commanded grace. The verb *command* sounds paradoxical in relation to grace, but Jill also commanded laughter, patience, togetherness, and action—just not while supine on her yoga mat.

"I love to hear you breathe," I told her one day as we dressed for class. By then, we had practiced yoga together for over a dozen years.

"I love that compliment!" exclaimed our teacher, Sara Jane Hayes, who was walking by and overheard.

Jill and I had both followed Sara Jane from prior studios, appreciating her expertise in alignment and her insights into why we make shapes of the body. But Jill, who had also driven out of town to take Sara Jane's classes, likened herself to a groupie.

It may have been Jill's love for our teacher that inspired her to exalt the room with those expansive, cleansing breaths. A beloved professor, Jill was also a model student, focusing her attention on the lessons to come and safeguarding space for Sara Jane to work.

No one recognized the value of holding space better than Jill, which she did repeatedly and often in private. She could make of herself a moment on behalf of another and show anyone who was interested in learning how to replicate the gesture. She taught generations of students as well as colleagues and friends how to offer words of alliance, understanding, or grief; how to turn those words into acts; how to protect silence. When we accept others as they are and where they are, fully, even if only for an hour—she knew—we route them toward self-assurance.

Such a lesson is invaluable, but it is only one part of a two-part course. I nearly missed the second lesson. Another day, another week, and the moment of instruction would have passed. As an educator, I am astonished by the chance operations of our educations—the real ones, in how to be. We may have read a dozen books on a subject or participated in twice as many discussions, but it's that one day we witness someone come to another's rescue when our paradigm shifts. Rarely can any of us trace the origins of our commitments to those who modeled them for us. Perhaps every class should end like a yoga class, by bowing to what we can and cannot see.

I only comprehended the second lesson months after walking into work one morning when my path met Jill's. A minute later, and I would have missed the opportunity to begin my day with her. Only after she was gone would I realize I would not get another. Here is the value of being open to every moment, and Jill's office door was open every time I sought her consultation, though I know she often closed it after me and countless others to whom she gave her full attention. Knowing when to close a door and when to open it—even when there are no doors under an open sky—is the key to holding space for others. Jill was able to wrap that time we had together in her presence because she cultivated hers. That morning she had been cultivating it by walking alone those blocks between her house and campus. Holding space for others begins by holding space for ourselves.

Sometimes that means taking a walk before work, and sometimes it means walking away from a situation until the tension passes, or we can change it. Widening our outreach requires fortifying personal boundaries. Sometimes there is nothing we can do but breathe deeply and refuse to abandon ourselves during some discomfort, which teachers say is why we practice yoga.

One Tuesday after Jill missed our regular class, I texted her a sunrise emoticon to share the rays I gathered for her, and she sent prayer mudra hands. Sara Jane ends most of her classes with this mudra and a Sanskrit mantra that translates as, "May all beings everywhere be happy and free." When Jill discovered she was struggling with more than a virus, I sent Deva Premal and Miten's sung rendition of this chant, *Lokah Samastah Sukhino Bhavantu*. On the recording, the duet communes with that wish Sara Jane offered to unite our hearts before we went our separate ways.

"Best gift!" Jill replied from a hospital bed. Her last words to me. This woman who authorized myriad individuals to express themselves, who could withhold judgment while bearing witness, who was surely entrusted with hundreds more secrets than she encouraged others to acknowledge via the Clothesline Project, who could turn herself into an ocean and draw in the tide. Such was her generosity of spirit.

Warrior
Haiku by Jolann Baldwin

86

Inspirational
Kind, loving, compassionate
You will be so missed

For Jill
Poetry by Lisa Sims

You loved us
And taught us about Self Love
You spoke for us
And taught us to Speak for Ourselves
You protected us
And showed us how to protect others

You helped us Unlearn
Centuries of Misogynistic Practices and Thinking

You helped us to See
The Beauty of Being
A Girl
A Woman
A Daughter, Mother, Friend, Partner, and Ally

You helped us to See
The Beauty of Being
Different
The Beauty of Being
Ourselves

You helped us to Understand
That Softness and Strength
Can exist in the same person
And
That Peace and Power
Can live wonderfully together

You guided us

Bohemian Earth Mother
Poetry by Wanda McNabb

You were a free spirit and
a bohemian earth mother
those who knew you were
your friends and many were
your admirers—soft and gentle
like the ocean breeze—
brilliant educator—
warm and trustworthy friend—
you were loved by many
of the human and furry types—
you will be missed by all your friends
and will be welcomed when you
return to mother earth in your
newly born body—
the fates will treat you well and
your kind soul will not be forgotten.
Thank you for your life, Jill

Jill Walked Beside Us
Nonfiction and Poetry by Kitty Madden

"There is nothing either good or bad, but thinking makes it so."
Shakespeare

A thought-provoking saying often attributed to Albert Camus was once sent to me by my older sister which read:
"Do not follow; I might not lead;
Do not lead; I might not follow;
Just walk beside me and be my friend."
Jill epitomized and embodied both these thoughts. Jill knew how to walk beside everyone as far as I could observe: her friends, her students, her spouse, and her children! She was non-judgmental. Even when Beverly and I both dropped her recorder music on the ground on two separate occasions, scattering her recorder music to the winds, she said, "That's okay, I need to put them in separate binders anyway."

She once asked for Reiki, claiming, "You are more souped up." Jill and I both paid a lot to become certified Reiki Masters. Her humility and engagement as a Reiki teacher were incomparable!

When Beverly and I sang a tribute to Mary Tyler Moore during Mary's death week, Jill sang with us and agreed: "We're gonna make it after all!"

Even If You Are

As Director of Women's Studies at APSU, Jill headed up the *Clothesline Project* for many years. One year, when it was outside near the flowing fountain and Olen Bryant's sculpture *The Sentinel*, often referred to as "The Green Man," Jill made a point of inviting me to make a T-shirt. I immediately chose lavender paint. It was a color that both Jill and I often gravitated toward. It didn't provide much contrast against the white T-shirt, but I guess my message struck a chord with Jill because she hugged me upon reading aloud: "EVEN IF YOU ARE A LESBIAN, WE'LL STILL LOVE YOU!" (Thanks, Ma.) Jill then said: "I love you because you're a lesbian!"

Titillating Breasts Exposed

Here's another prominent memory of Jill. She and Barry had invited me and Beverly to a solstice party (I think it was) along with several friends, including Nancy Telford, the Reiki Master Teacher who attuned me and Jill. As an "Earth Mother," Jill breastfed four-year-old Hannah in the middle of their couch in the midst of the party. Jill gaily related a story of walking around their house with her shirt open to "air out" her breasts. One day a UPS employee got his *own* story to tell when Jill opened the door, forgetting to button her shirt!

Pretend It's Play
Reflections on the first of the august performers of '57
Jill Elizabeth Eichhorn!

You saw opportunities to radiate Eve Ensler's *The Vagina Monologues* into the world through your avid participation, inspiration, and raw encouragement. You helped immerse her famous play into the culture of Roxy Regional Theatre and Austin Peay State University.

You saw that your children, Ted and Hannah, are truly unique, brilliant—even defiant—individuals. When Hannah suggested that we all go swimming in the eternal reflecting pool at Cheekwood Gardens, you gently explained that we can't this time. When Hannah exclaimed, "There's no sign that says we can't!" You laughed heartily, saying, "My children need a sign!"

Pretend it's play!

When you lay dying with Hannah and Barry at your sides, I wonder if you wondered if you must make way for your first grandson, Elliot Arthur Kitterman—born just days after you died.

Pretend it's play!

Pretense remains reality because pretense becomes reality! Play your recorder with abandon, Jill!

And pretend it's a play.

The Be-Keeping of Friendship

They say that to have a friend,
One must be a friend,
And when you befriend a friend,
You must let that friend be a friend.
And to let that friend be a friend,
You must let that friend be.

That was Jill.

Learning to Love

It's August 1. Today Jill E. Eichhorn would have been 66, had she "hung on" long enough to "meet and greet" her only grandchild (so far), whom her son, Ted, and daughter-in-law, Hannah, named Elliot Arthur Kitterman. The name "Arthur" honors his grandfather, Barry Arthur Kitterman. Some friends have suggested that Jill left this earth plane so quickly after hearing her dreaded stage IV diagnosis to make way for Elliot to receive most of his loved ones' attentions as newborns always deserve! I myself hinted at that with loved ones in an adapted song about Jill.

Long ago when I was still Hannah's trusted nanny, Jill came over as Beverly, Hannah, and I were watching *Groundhog Day*. Jill proclaimed, "Oh, we've seen that before; it's one of the good ones." So I offered her Reiki (as a "sister" Reiki Master), and she accepted it on a healing table in our living room. Beverly and Hannah finished processing the obvious metaphors of Bill Murray's character dying over and over and over again until he finally learned to love.

Eagle

When my sister, Mary Alaina, died in December 2002, and my sister, Ann, died in December 2018, and Luna the wonder dog with the HUGE HEART (literally and figuratively) died Thanksgiving weekend of 2021, Jill wrote down Joy Harjo's "Eagle Poem" in her beautiful cards. The added benefit with Luna was that Jill actually brought her recorder to play near Luna's grave, and then she graced us with a recital of Harjo's poem by heart.

We love all your memories, beloved Jill, and thank you from the bottom of all of our hearts for recording in our consciousness and sharing so many memories with all of us!

Lucid Dream

Beverly, Ann, Mary Alaina, Chi Chi, and I were playing a "game" in a beautiful living room with roses *everywhere*—even woven into an antique wool rug—when Jill arrived to take us to an event at Austin Peay State University. We explained our game, which was: "Imagine you are here thinking of what, *exactly* you wish to be doing and whom you want to be with while you are doing it." Then we got into a TANK of a car, and Jill got into the back, expecting Beverly to drive. The car started driving *itself*, and I, Kitty, yelled out, "Star!" I mean, "Steer!" Then, Beverly became the extremely careful, hyper-aware driver that she really is.

Note: Three of these souls are currently "dead." The other three still abide on this earth literally (as far as I know). All of our "other" loved ones are not literally *in* this love poem, but they were all there!

I am here,
You are there.
We can be everywhere if we dare.
Jill is now here, there, and everywhere.

I Want to be Catlike
Poetry by Bryanna Licciardi

*Cats teach us that not everything in nature has a purpose**
and I want to say fuck your purpose. I want to cherry–
     pick you apart
and bat your pieces around the floor.
I want my tail to flick-flick, a sign to back off
     and chill.

Flip of a switch from absent-minded to neurosis focus.
Cats divinize the room,
prayer hands smooth over their backs.
What I want is to touch my throat and say,
     I'm empty here, please help.

Let me, or else, watch
as I envelop their self-desire.

**First line taken from Garrison Keillor.*

Maestro's Funeral
Nonfiction by Beverly Fisher

Maestro the cat had the unique position in our vast menagerie of being one of the few pets to die naturally at home. Unfortunately, he started going downhill on a Thanksgiving weekend, which meant little chance of finding a veterinarian to help send him on his way. Thankfully, he died peacefully.

We called Jill about his passing because all the Eichhorn/Kittermans (but especially Ted and Hannah) knew Maestro very well. Kitty was Ted and Hannah's nanny, and the children had spent many days interacting with all our animals. Nine-year-old Hannah knew the feeding routine so well that we hired her to take care of the animals when we went on vacation. Of course, she was driven by a parent, but Hannah was the one who knew the routine of feeding seven animals. It is a tribute to Jill and Barry that when Kitty was listing everything that needed to be done to take care of the animals, Kitty asked, "Hannah, what is the most important thing to remember," expecting Hannah to say, "Water." Hannah said, "Love."

After calling Jill and telling her about Maestro, all the Eichhorn/Kittermans arrived within the hour, barely giving us enough time to dig a grave. We all stood around the site, crying, singing, and sharing memories of our furry family member. So not only had Jill and her family blessed us with laughter on many occasions, but they knew how to mourn with us and share their comfort. So, our Thanksgiving weekend was filled with giving thanks on that occasion and on many occasions for the kindness of Jill, Barry, Ted, and Hannah.

Hannah and the Tree of Life
Haiku by blue Bastin

95

I knew your smile first
Then I met her and could tell
Where you got it from

Your Heart Next to Mine
Poetry by Wanda McNabb

I was shocked to find out
Surprised I hadn't been told
About your illness after all I
Told you about mine but then
You were a private person and
Often quiet about your personal
Life—but never quiet about the
Passions in your life—women's
Rights and reproductive rights
And standing up against the tyranny
That was chauvinistic bull-hockey.
Knowing you made me stand a little
Taller, believe in myself and know
That I had value in my life. I will miss
You coming to visit me and inquiring
How I was, sharing a meal at Jasmin's.
I will miss your kind heart but know
I will have it beating next to mine for
The rest of my days, if only in memory.
My dear friend, I will remember you always.
Jill.

When All the Bullshit Fades Away
Nonfiction by Denise Galben

The first time I truly connected with Jill was after a service at the Unitarian Universalist fellowship about six years ago. She approached me and asked me about my dancing and was genuinely interested. Noted. She asked me how long I had been dancing, and I told her that I didn't start dancing until my late 30s. She asked me why I danced, as was her way of making people think about themselves in the process of self-discovery. I told her that it had saved me from a very dark place, and that I don't really care what people think about me being a dancer who is old(er). She looked at me and said, "I love it when all the bullshit falls away, when older women can finally be who they're supposed to be." She said it with passion, and perhaps a tinge of anger. She seemed satisfied with all of my answers, as if she were sharing my victory with me. This, *this*, is how I remember Jill.

Tributes to Jill

Jill shared this philosophy with me: "I always try to think of the kindest thing to say."—Mya Rachlin

In our journey through life, we meet special people. I consider Jill one of those special people. She had a light that shined and just grabbed you. Sharing a friendship with Jill made me want to be a better person. I consider it a gift that I shared a friendship with Jill.—Cynthia Fitch

I am so saddened by the sudden loss of Dr. Jill Eichhorn! She was my advisor during all of my undergraduate years at Austin Peay. She was kind, supportive, and nurturing. She is the reason I was enrolled in the honors program my freshman year. At every advising session, she always encouraged me to practice self care, and to relish the college experience as a time for exploration and extracurricular activity—even if that meant taking fewer classes.

I recall with fondness the water tank in her office; one time during an advising session she poured water in a Ball jar for me to drink, and stated that we all need more water. This actual act of care has taken on symbolic significance in my psyche. While a simple act, the water-giving conveyed much.

I had the pleasure of hearing from her a few weeks ago, and I cherish that she sent me a message. I know her influence has been felt among many lives, and it will continue to be felt as all of us hand down lessons we learned from her. —Charles Knight. *Facebook - Monday, October 3, 2022, at 5:05 p.m.*

I've been mustering up the strength to write these words so bear with me starting at the beginning:

It's 2007, three weeks into my first semester of college, and I've just found out that my schedule is a mess. I'm registered for classes that don't count and classes that I apparently already have credit for. I drop as many as I can, but there is one I'm sad to drop—my English Comp course—because there's something about the professor, Dr. Jill Eichhorn, that warms my heart. She was energetic, intelligent, quirky, and enigmatic. I decide to approach her in the hall to tell her I was leaving the class. This is so not like me. I'm extremely shy. She says she's sorry to see me go and asks if I have an advisor yet. I don't. She tells me if I change my major to English she would be honored to advise me. I like her so much already that I decide to change majors on a whim and say, "Sure, why not!"

That conversation in the hallway changed me for the better. Because of Jill, I did things I didn't think I was brave enough to do over the next four years—discovering I was a feminist, sharing my poetry with people, performing a skit about pubic hair on stage for charity. Jill's passion for equality and literature bonded me to her well beyond our time together in the classroom. It's been fifteen years since that hallway, and she's shown up for me every step of the way—prepping for interviews, writing recommendations for graduate school, attending my wedding, my book signing. Most recently, she came to my doctoral graduation party with Barry. Only weeks ago, we were sitting down with margaritas in some beautiful weather, reflecting on our friendship over the years. I didn't know that would be our last moment together.

It's impossible to express the loss of Jill. But it's important to attempt to, anyway, because I am now an educator myself. It's important to remember that there are teachers out there who change lives, who carry tremendous power in their small acts of kindness. You are so loved and admired, Jill. —Bryanna Licciardi. *Facebook – Tuesday, October 4, 2022.*

Wisdom of Jill
Nonfiction by Beverly Fisher

One way Jill served the world was to listen carefully and give wise advice. I share a few of her words of wisdom.

"Food is for nourishment." This phrase from Jill came from a workshop she gave about food. She said, "Food is for nourishment." Simple, yet to me at that time, profound. Having money in the land of giant supermarkets of plenty, I realized that my eating of potato chips, brownies, and fried chicken was not based on nourishment. Though I haven't given up my favorite foods, because of Jill's words and demonstration (just think of her refrigerator drawers overflowing with fresh produce) I have added many more fruits and vegetables to my diet. I so associate Jill with healthful eating that, after her death, I found myself swirling in a vortex of indecision in the produce section of Kroger. I could not decide what to buy, yet I could not leave the fruits and vegetables. I stayed so long the employees were staring at me. Was I in the episode of *Buffy the Vampire Slayer* where no one could leave the house? Was Jill holding me there, trying to save me from the aisles of pre-packaged foods filled with mysterious, slow-poisoning ingredients? Or was my grief so intense or my search for solace so fierce, they tethered me to what Jill advocated? That's all unknown, but I still think of Jill in the produce section of any store or when viewing gardens filled with nourishing, soul-sustaining and life-enhancing manna.

"It's not rational." Many times, when I tried to get Jill's take on an episode in my life, she would say, "It's not rational." My anguish would fall away, and I was relieved of the burden of trying to make sense of it all and think, "Oh, yeah." Jill's succinct observation brought me back to some rationality of my own.

"Choose your battles." Jill used this phrase especially when her children were young, but it is very apt to use at any age. I took it to mean that one doesn't *have* to fight over everything. Jump into the chaos or let it float away—a choice that Jill seemed to skillfully navigate.

"I just had a different idea." One expression that I have spent a lot of time thinking about is "I just had a different idea." Jill was describing to me a dispute she had had with someone which had gotten ugly. Weeks later, Jill's analysis was that the other person had not accepted that Jill simply had a different idea of what needed to be done. That struck me and made me realize that at times I, too, did not accept the different idea of another person (see "choose your battles" above). Because of Jill, I have tried to accept respectfully the different ideas of others. Admittedly, putting that idea into practice has been sometimes elusive, but I strive to remember it.

"Be Like Jill." One of Jill's talented students created products with the saying, "Be Like Jill." I found that expression to be so touching and apropos. If only we could "Be Like Jill," our world would be filled with joy, love, thoughtfulness, peace, kindness, appreciation, and wonder. Yes, we would all do well to be like Jill, think like Jill, and love like Jill. I hope a few sayings of Jill will help us all remember to do just that.

Options
Nonfiction by Marna Maldavs

Sometimes there are no right solutions to bad situations. There are only options.

I was delivering pizzas one night. I pulled into a drive and heard yelling. It sounded male, and it sounded angry. It stopped after I closed my car door. I went to the door and knocked. I heard nothing. I waited. Nothing. I knocked a little harder.

A woman opened the door. She had been crying. One side of her face was red, and she was holding her arm at the elbow. It was obvious she had just been a victim of domestic violence.

I asked her if she was okay. She shook her head no. I asked her if I should call the police. She shook her head no.

I asked her if she wanted to get in my car. I told her I could take her somewhere safe. She hesitated. She gave it seconds of thought. She shook her head no.

She paid for the pizza. She winced from the pain in her arm the weight of the pizza caused.

The transaction weighed on me. *Was the woman all right? How was she going to explain her injuries to her family and friends? Did she live in fear? Did I do the right thing? Should I have called the police? Would that have made her situation worse?* It was weighing on me a few days later when I saw Jill at the UU.

I did not approach Jill. Jill approached me. She could tell something was wrong. I told her what I had witnessed and how I reacted. She listened. She did not judge. She did not give me advice. She gave me empathy and support. Then, miraculously, and out of nowhere, she produced a pamphlet for a local women's shelter. It was on her person. What kind of person has a pamphlet for a local women's shelter for the ready? Jill.

I thanked Jill for her empathetic ears, her support, and the pamphlet. I put the pamphlet in my glove box, hoping I would never need it.

A couple weeks later, I had a delivery to the same address as before. I took the pamphlet out of the glove box and put it in my pocket. The same woman answered the door. No one else in sight, I offered her the pamphlet. She took it. She folded it and put it in her back pocket.

I never saw the woman again. I don't know if she got out of her bad situation. All I know is that because of Jill, she had an option.

Those She Never Knew
Poetry by Tyler Nolting

She made a lasting impact
Her imprint can't be matched
She fought for rights of others
Their hearts and souls she patched

Students were her calling
To mold and help refine
The shiny pearl or diamond
That she saw inside

Violence she opposed
Of body and the mind
She raised up victims' voices
Hung their words on a line

The airing out of truths
And the love within her heart
Were a kryptonite for hate
And made her life a work of art

An angel left this earth
She did all she could do
Her pebble ripples selfless love
To those she never knew

Earth Mother
For Jill
Poetry by Mitzi Cross

When I heard of your passing,
I had to sit down
and pull my wind back to me.
I closed my eyes squeezing
the salt running into my ears.

I couldn't wash
the image out of my mind,
of a giant, felled, sentient Redwood.

I could hear a slow, whispering,
blue, rain on some lonely
mountaintop in the Rockies.

I could hear the crackling
under the ice of a frozen
lake in Montana.

Everything felt slower,
even the murmuration of starlings,
sailing in and out of heart formations,
infinity symbols, a swan, all moving
in slow symphony across the sun
but I was moon-burned
with insomnia.

The next day I took a long hike,
pouring my pain out in my sweat,
pushing my muscles to swell,
and I remember how sure-footed
you were on a hike, how lean your

calves were as they stormed up the trail
in front of me, a warrior woman, fifteen
years my senior and I struggled
to keep up. I made a joke at my
expense and you tossed your head back
in deep, untethered, belly laughs,
which only encouraged me to keep going.

ABOUT THE CONTRIBUTORS

Editorial Board

Beverly Fisher is a retired attorney. She is the author of *Grace Among the Leavings* (Thorncraft Publishing, 2013) which has been made into a one-act and a two-act play. A play she wrote, *Daddy Said He* was performed at the Roxy Regional Theatre in June 2019.

Barbara Lee Gray—I am an instructor of English and Women's and Gender Studies at APSU as well as a musician and songwriter. Over the past twenty years, I participated both onstage and off in many performances of *The Vagina Monologues*.

Jennifer Goode Stevens has been editing for more than thirty years: newspapers, magazines, books, websites, blogs, ads, restaurant menus, and the occasional egregious roadside marquee. She is a senior copy editor at Vanderbilt University and lives in Clarksville with her husband, two teenagers, and a dog.

Shana Thornton is the author of three novels, *Ripe for the Pickin'* (2021), *Poke Sallet Queen and the Family Medicine Wheel* (2015), and *Multiple Exposure* (2012), as well as a children's chapter book *The Adventures to Pawnassus* (2019). She is co-author of the nonfiction self-help book *Seasons of Balance: On Creativity and Mindfulness* (2016). Shana earned an M.A. in English from Austin Peay State University. She is the Montgomery County deputy historian, the founder of the Clarksville Montgomery County African American Legacy Trail (est. 2019), and a longtime board member of the Friends of Dunbar Cave Inc. Visit thorncraftpublishing.com for more info.

Cover Designer: Dr. Cynthia Marsh is a narrative artist. She uses words and found imagery to translate contemporary conversations into books, prints, and broadsides.

Ms. Marsh was educated at Moore College of Art, Rochester Institute of Technology, and the larger world that informs our ideas. She was a founding member of the Graphic Center @ the Woman's Building in LA. Throughout the 1980's, her studio produced prints and illustrations for the entertainment industry. Marsh held teaching positions at California State University, Northridge, Otis College of Art + Design, and Austin Peay State University. At APSU, she founded the Goldsmith Press—a working museum of wood type that encouraged community members to print and post their stories.

Contributing Authors and Artists

blue Bastin—a person who creates art in between the art of living from day to day.

Beatrix Brockman is professor of German and the chair of the Department of Languages and Literature at Austin Peay State University. She met Jill Eichhorn when she immigrated to the United States in 2002 from Germany. Jill Eichhorn was Brockman's professor throughout her B.A. and M.A. degrees at APSU, and, when Dr. Brockman returned as a professor, Jill became her mentor and cherished friend.

Susan Calovini is a retired academic who served as an English professor and college administrator at institutions in three states, including at Austin Peay State University. She earned a bachelor's degree in journalism from Ohio University and graduate degrees in English from the Ohio State University. During her career, she taught literature, writing, and women's studies; published and presented her research on nineteenth- and twentieth-century women writers; and held various leadership positions, including department chair, college dean, and vice president for academic affairs. She currently resides in Winston-Salem, North Carolina.

Cindy Smith Chambers is a lifelong writer and award-winning instructor. A former Polish linguist in Military Intelligence, Chambers has held a number of communication roles in her lengthy professional life. She was a section editor of the *Fort Campbell Courier*, wrote a weekly humor column for the international newspaper *The Stars & Stripes*, was head of public relations at Clarksville Academy, and served as creative director for a local ad agency for nearly 10 years. She has hosted radio and TV shows, is a Distinguished Toastmaster, and most recently held the position of PR director and full-time faculty member for Bethel University, where she taught College Writing for more than fifteen years. She holds an A.A., a B.S., and an MBA; since retirement, she has served as a volunteer tutor for the local Adult Literacy Council's English as a Second Language program. A proud mother of two and grandmother of one, Chambers enjoys gardening, cooking, reading, decorating, exercising, painting, playing trivia, and making excuses for her two dogs' crazy behavior.

Daniel Christian was first mesmerized by the soothing presence and teaching style of Jill in 2002 when he went with his mother, Aleeta, to Jill's yoga class during lunch at Austin Peay State University. Daniel's mother Aleeta, and his father Floyd, worked with Jill and Barry Kitterman at APSU. Daniel further connected with Jill over the years at various opportunities on the campus of APSU and at the Unitarian Universalist Fellowship Clarksville, where Daniel began directing music in 2002 and continues today. Jill has always been a guiding light for Daniel in the community and at the fellowship, where the two shared a weekly musical journey, intimately working together, and sharing emails and phone texts to plan and provide musical experiences for the Fellowship. Jill always continued to expand her recorder playing skills, and eagerly made learning something new and an almost childlike experience. In planning the music at the church services, there was not a week over the past nearly ten years that Daniel did not think through how Jill might enjoy trying something new to play and grow in some way, perhaps in effort from Daniel to give back to Jill in reflection of her deep impact on Daniel's life. Daniel has taken precious memories of moments he cherishes with Jill with him into his life projects, such as his mind and body wellness practices as well as his current career working with older adults in a caregiving setting, providing art, music, and meditative experiences. Daniel continues to learn new things and grow, remembering to breathe, forever with a mindset affected lovingly by the tenderness of Jill Eichhorn.

Mitzi Cross is a playwright, poet, novelist, and fine-art photographer. Her writing and photography have appeared in several publications throughout the South. Most recently, three of her photographs appeared in the Manifest gallery's catalog titled *The New Nude*. Mitzi is a Reiki Master and a practitioner of Healing Touch. Spirit has guided her to be a conduit for healing and working specifically with sexual abuse survivors and survivors of domestic violence. She has led memoir writing, poetry, and creative writing groups for over twenty years and is completely dedicated to using her writing, photography, energy medicine, yoga, guided imagery, and integrative breathwork to assist others along his or her path to becoming one's authentic self.

Bo (aka Flowers) Fowler was a student at APSU from August of 2018 to December of 2023. He is the co-founder of the student organization called "The Peacemakers" which is devoted to the betterment of campus & the World. He is now a teacher and a freelance animator.

Denise Galben is a native of Clarksville and met Jill many years ago at the Unitarian Universalist Fellowship. Denise occasionally writes poetry and does spoken word, but her main creative outlet is dance and movement. She has several jobs and wears many hats. She considers her children to be her life's greatest accomplishment.

Joanna Grisham (most folx call her Joey) holds an MFA in creative writing from Georgia College. She recently won the Carnegie Center for Literacy & Learning's Next Great Writers Contest and was a semifinalist for *The MacGuffin's* Poet Hunt 28 contest. She was a finalist for the 2021-2022 Very Short Fiction Contest at the Tennessee Williams & New Orleans Literary Festival and a finalist for the 2021 Ember Chasm Review Flash Fiction Contest. Her work has appeared in *On the Run, Still: The Journal, Gleam, The Emerson Review, The Write Launch*, and other places, and her first chapbook of poems, *Phantoms*, was published by Finishing Line Press in November 2023. She lives in Tennessee with her wife and daughter and teaches at Austin Peay State University.

Valerie M. Guzman: Before being named CEO of the United Way of the Greater Clarksville Region in 2019, Guzman worked as a client service and outreach coordinator for the Sexual Assault Center, a partner agency of UWGCR. The positions allowed her to develop and maintain a community leadership presence for SAC in the city and surrounding areas.

Guzman served two four-year terms, 2012-2020, as a city councilperson, and as Mayor Pro-Tem 2016-2018, for the city of Clarksville. Her chief responsibilities were communicating policies and programs to residents, responding to constituent needs and complaints, and representing the community to other levels of government. Guzman was also a small business owner responsible for the company's direction. She was in charge of creating and managing the business plan, developing their marketing campaigns, and constructing ways to keep the business competitive and profitable.

Guzman earned a bachelor of science degree from Bethel University, focusing on management and organizational development, where she was awarded magna cum laude. She also currently serves on the following boards throughout the community: board president of Montgomery County Library Foundation; board president on the City of Clarksville Sustainability Board; Clarksville-Montgomery County Planning Commission; Bella's Closet board member; and Eagle Scout panelist.

Tami Haaland met Jill Eichhorn in graduate school many years ago, and the two maintained their friendship through busy lives and sometimes long silences. Haaland is the author of three poetry collections, including *What Does Not Return*, *When We Wake in the Night*, and *Breath in Every Room*. Her poems have appeared recently in *The American Journal of Poetry*, *Cutthroat*, *december*, and *Cascadia*, and have been featured on *The Writer's Almanac*, *Verse Daily*, *American Life in Poetry*, and *The Slowdown*.

Jordan Hoekstra is a native of Clarksville, Tennessee. She attended Austin Peay State University, where she received her bachelor's degree in professional studies with a minor in women's and gender studies. While attending APSU, she was named to the 2015 Who's Who Among Students in American Universities and Colleges, received the Betty Joe Wallace Women's Studies Activist Award within the Women and Gender Studies Program, and served as the President for Feminist Majority Leadership Alliance. She currently works as a clinical administrator for Guided Path Counseling. Hoekstra lives in Clarksville with her wonderful husband, William, and their two precious boys, Adam and Nathan. Hoekstra enjoys time with her family, sweet tea and coffee, being a part of her church, and constantly wanting to learn and grow.

Tracy Jepson has been working as a public historian in Tennessee for over a decade. She earned her M.A. in history at the University of Memphis, with a focus on the social and cultural history of the United States. While working at a Civil War site in Tennessee, she met and partnered with Frederick Deshon Murphy to create The Tennessee African American Historical Group. The group's mission is to provide fresh research concerning previously unknown histories and share them through traveling exhibitions, presentations, and documentaries. In her personal life, she loves hiking and traveling with her husband, Brian, and spending time with their three grown children.

Charles Knight (Chuck) holds an M.S. in Information Sciences from the University of Tennessee (2023) and a B.A. in English from Austin Peay State University (2005). After working for sixteen years in employee benefits, he is making a career change to become a librarian. In his free time, he enjoys being in the company of his husband and two cats, reading, watching good TV shows, and seeing films at Nashville's arthouse cinema gem, The Belcourt.

Bryanna Licciardi is an educator and writer, with an MFA in poetry and a doctorate in education. She's the author of poetry chapbook *Skin Splitting* (Finishing Line Press, 2017) and the collection *Fish Love* (Alternating Current Press, 2024). When not teaching or writing, she plays cat mom to four rescues and wife to one musician husband. Check out her work at www.bryannalicciardi.com.

Wanda McNabb: I am a writer, poet, playwright, actress, and musician. I worked for APSU and got to know Jill through my work in the Lang/Lit office. We became friends during that time, and when I retired and moved to Murray, Jill and Barry came to visit me. Jill was a dear friend and someone I hope I see again soon in the afterlife or when she reincarnates. She had much more work to do to be taken from us so suddenly. She inspired so many of us to live our lives to the fullest that knowing her was invaluable to our survival as women. Hers was a gentle spirit, and yet she was so fierce an advocate for women's rights. I will always remember her kind smile and her laugh. I will always miss her.

Kitty Madden has been known as Thorncraft's literary midwife, bringing out the best writing from many authors. Kitty was once a professional proofreader, nanny, and substitute teacher. She is currently a Reiki Master, practicing in Clarksville, Tennessee. She lives in sacred woods connected to ancient, petrified coral-strewn streams. She practices continually singing healing tones, coaxing dancing waters from a Tibetan dragon bowl with Chi Chi, a dependent, resplendent, transcending, ascending, canine Reiki Master. She is the inspiration for a YouTube channel, "Kooky Kitty and Luna C. Bass," as well as co-creator, contributor, and co-producer.

Terry Morris is a long-time friend of Jill. He is a member of the Unitarian Universalist Fellowship and the Director of the Clarksville Montgomery County African American Legacy Trail. He earned a Bachelor of Music from the University of Memphis and an MBA from Bethel University.

Tyler Nolting: I am an assistant professor of public health, in the Department of Health and Human Performance at Austin Peay State University (APSU). I have been teaching public health courses at the university level since 2007. I received all of my education from Indiana University, earning my Bachelor of Science degree in Kinesiology with an emphasis in Exercise Science (minor in Spanish), a Master of Public Health degree, and a Doctor of Philosophy in Health Behavior, with a minor in Human Performance. I am also a Master-Certified Health Education Specialist®.

I am married to Paola Zurita Valdebenito, from Chile, and a Spanish instructor in APSU's Department of Languages and Literature. We have two children, Isabella and Leo. I never met Dr. Jill Eichhorn, but after hearing her life stories after her passing, I felt like I knew her well enough to write the poem "Those She Never Knew."

Lisa Sims grew up in San Antonio, Texas, and Germany. While in Germany, she was blessed to travel Europe. She has also been able to visit family in Canada and Mexico. Her next travel goal is to visit more of her mother's family in Romania. Lisa lives in South Korea where she teaches English as a second language.

Yoga and meditation have played an enormous part in her ability to heal, as have Taiji and Qigong. The combination of these practices have also led her into a healthier relationship with herself and her mother. Sims credits her aptitude for deeply diving into these ancient practices and their teachings with her ability to reconcile with her mother; to enjoy a peaceful, loving relationship with her mom before she passed away early in 2020. Sims also believes everything she's learned through practicing yoga, Taiji, and Qigong has helped her to be a better mother, a better grandmother, and a better version of herself. She is grateful to the teachers at Yoga Mat and Stuart Bonnington for their guidance and patience.

Rediscovering her love of and talent for writing is also a direct result of Sims's yoga, Taiji, and Qigong practices. They are also what helped her to recognise the courage to bare herself to others through her writing. These ancient practices have done for her exactly what has been written about them for hundreds of years: revealed her true self to herself—a self worthy of love.

Shauna Snyder was born in 1982 in middle West Virginia, having moved to Middle Tennessee in 2003 at the age of 21. She graduated from Austin Peay State University in 2010 with a B.A. in psychology with a minor in music (vocal) and in 2012 with an M.S. in psychology/counseling.

Snyder volunteered years of support to pregnancy and infant loss support groups while coping with her own fertility struggles eventually blessing her with a beautiful daughter, Viviana, in 2015. In 2020, covid left her with mast cell activation syndrome sparking her to help increase access quality health care for this rare and isolating autoimmune disease. She can most often be found reading mystery novels. She is a mother, counselor, poetry/songwriter, cat enthusiast, and friend. She enjoyed over twenty years with her beloved late calico cat, Roxie. For information on current progress on original literary works, follow Snyder at patreon.com/writeitinmysoul

Lachon Sumers is a Tennessee native and has been writing since she was eight-years-old. Sumers' writing for Thorncraft Publishing will be her first time having her work published in print. "Every Woman

Should Be a Feminist" and "Before I Was a Feminist" are two bodies of work that address the unspoken and unknowns of feminism, while honoring the life of the one who taught her about feminism. When Sumers is not writing, she is reading and enjoying conversations of her peers. She hopes to write more in her future. Sumers's blog: https://lachonsbk.wixsite.com/lachon-sumers

Dr. Mickey Wadia serves in the Department of Languages and Literature at Austin Peay State University in Clarksville, Tennessee. A Shakespearean scholar by discipline, he also teaches technical writing courses and other classes within the Honors Program. He frequently presents guest lectures on Shakespeare to students in the Clarksville-Montgomery County School System and Houston County schools. He has been invited as a scholar/speaker for Insight Talks preceding performances of Shakespeare plays by the Nashville Shakespeare Festival. Wadia is the recipient of APSU's two most prestigious teaching awards: The Socrates Award (1996) for teaching excellence by junior untenured faculty and the National Alumni Association Distinguished Professor Award (2007). He was elected as the faculty representative to the APSU Board of Trustees and served for two years from July 2019 through June 2021. He also served as president of the Faculty Senate from May 2018 - May 2019.

A London travel veteran and study abroad expert, Wadia has taken hundreds of students and community members to London, Scotland, Ireland, and Australia in his capacity as board trustee for CCSA (Cooperative Center for Study Abroad). In June 2019, he was invited to teach a Shakespeare class in London and Paris (May - June 2019) for the Catalyst study abroad program. He was also invited as the faculty leader to accompany APSU alumni in their travels to England, Scotland, Wales, Switzerland, Austria, and Bavaria.

Courtney Woodard is a social worker and a former student of Dr. Jill Eichhorn. Woodard achieved her bachelor's in social work with minors in women's and gender studies and African-American studies from Austin Peay State University. She went on to achieve her master's in social work from the University of South Carolina.

Woodard works as a social worker at Nashville State Community College, where she helps students overcome barriers to earning a college education. Woodard enjoys reading, watching movies, and playing with her dogs. She is passionate about breaking barriers for women in education and hopes to carry on Jill's teachings to new generations.

Amy Wright co-edited and introduced the Virginia volume of *The Southern Poetry Anthology* and served as the 2022 Wayne G. Basler Chair of Excellence at East Tennessee State University. She has authored three poetry books and six chapbooks and received two Peter Taylor Fellowships to the Kenyon Review Writers Workshop, an Individual Artist Grant from the Tennessee Arts Commission, and a fellowship to the Virginia Center for the Creative Arts. Her nonfiction debut, *Paper Concert: A Conversation in the Round*, (Sarabande Books) won the 2022 Nautilus Gold Award for Lyric Prose.

Be
like
Jill.